Southern Cheyenne
Women's Songs

Southern Cheyenne Women's Songs

By Virginia Giglio

With a Foreword by David P. McAllester

UNIVERSITY OF OKLAHOMA PRESS
Norman and London

This book is published with the generous assistance of Edith Gaylord Harper.

Library of Congress Cataloging-in-Publication Data
Giglio, Virginia, 1953-
    Southern Cheyenne women's songs / by Virginia Giglio : with a foreword by David P. McAllester.—1st ed.
        p.   cm.
    Includes bibliographical references (p.   ) and index.
    Includes 36 songs.
    ISBN 0-8061-2605-1 (alk. paper)
    1. Cheyenne Indians—Music—History and criticism. 2. Cheyenne Indians—Women—Songs and music—History and criticism. 3. Folk music—Oklahoma—History and criticism. 4. Folk songs, Cheyenne—Oklahoma—History and criticism. 5. Women—Songs and music. 6. Cheyenne Indians—Women—Folklore. I. Title.
    ML3557.G53   1994
    782.42162'973—dc20   93-23221
                                                                          CIP
                                                                          MN

Text design by Cathy Carney Imboden.

1 2 3 4 5 6 7 8 9 10

To Barnabas and Daniel

Contents

Illustrations

PHOTOGRAPHS

Foreword
By David P. McAllester

It is my privilege to tell tales out of school, tales that it would not be seemly for the author of this book to tell about herself. Dr. Giglio's fieldwork for this study was an unusual case where a scholar stepped out of academe into a family circle. Her work was not conducted with "subjects" or "informants" but with "singer/consultants," a happy phrase indicating that *they* were the performers and the authorities. They opened their homes and their hearts to her, and *their* book brings to the reading public valuable insights into the everyday joys, aspirations, and sorrows of contemporary Cheyenne life. Dr. Giglio became a member of a Cheyenne family, an officer of one of the Benefit Societies, a sponsor of benefit dances, and an honored guest, many times, at the great annual Sun Dance, the spiritual peak of the Cheyenne year.

When Dr. Giglio's research culminated in the defense of the doctoral dissertation from which this book was drawn, a large body of Cheyenne supporters appeared to defend the defender. They spoke eloquently of Dr. Giglio's sympathetic understanding of their lives; at the party, afterwards, an honoring song had been prepared for the occasion. This is empathy: Dr. Giglio's appreciation of her Cheyenne friends and "relatives" and their culture is explicit in every page of her book and, as I observed, is mirrored by their appreciation of her. Her volatile laughter and tears were as important to her understanding of

Cheyenne daily life as were her linguistic studies, her musical analyses, her exploration of the previous literature and her skill at weaving all this material together.

"Anthropology" and "ethnomusicology" spelled out their blindness in the very polysyllabification with which they armed themselves against any taint of human sympathies. We now are beginning to see that classic "fieldwork" told us more about the investigator than it did about the people being studied. The depiction of people, not as they are but as they might have been at some imagined more "authentic" period of their history, the study of great men, the analysis of state and ceremonial occasions, are predilections of dominating cultures. From Plutarch's *Lives* to the latest biography of Sitting Bull we have clouded our vision with captains, kings, battles, bishops, and defenestrations.

Humanistic anthropology has refocused our vision on real people and everyday lives. "Reflexive" anthropology has encouraged an honest confession of our own feelings in our contacts with the other. Feminist anthropology has reminded us that there might be something in women's lives that we need to know in order to understand at least half of the cultural reality. Dr. Giglio's book takes us straightforwardly into all three of these dimensions of Cheyenne lives; in the process it gives us the gift of some delightful music.

A broad gamut of songs is presented here. There are the brief, easily learned melodies of the lullabies, with their evocative haiku-like texts. They make their appearance for the first time here in the literature on the Cheyenne. They take us from the expression of a mother's feelings to the legend of the mud hen. Equally compact but leading further into religion and mythology are the hand game songs with their mention of crow and magpie who helped humankind at the beginning of the world. There are melodic and textual clues to connections with the great song repertoire of Ghost Dance music. Dr. Giglio is satisfyingly aware of the importance of the textual component of song. We are given the Cheyenne as it would be spoken and as it is sung, followed by sensitive translations and discussions of the meaning of the songs in their cultural context.

The complex and extended war songs and social songs give us another dimension of Cheyenne thought and musical creativity. We move to extended and poignant statements on the meaning of life and death and to gusty excursions of humor.

The "spiritual" songs, in the context of everyday songs of women, turn out to be hymns, both traditional and newly composed. The striking change from straight, rapid rhythms to slow and long-held note-values alerts us to new elements in the musical repertoire. Even newer are the compositions of Joan Swallow set to Omnichord accompaniments. This tinkling electronic Japanese musical device, with its "boom-chuck" bass, adds Western European musical idioms, from East Asia, to the emerging Cheyenne mix.

In taking us into unexplored areas of Cheyenne music, past and present, Dr. Giglio has also given us a stimulating introduction to the Cheyenne creative imagination.

Preface

This book began the day I met Diane Hawk. I walked into her welcoming household one summer day in 1989, visiting her family as part of a group of students from the Summer Field School in Ethnology of the University of Oklahoma. The Hawks were busy preparing for the Southern Cheyenne sun dance ceremony to be held the next week at Seiling, Oklahoma, but took time to show the students some of their dance regalia and invited us to visit them at their camp at the sun dance. "Just look for the black truck with the silver trim, and come to the tent," they said. "You can't miss it."

That Oklahoma saying, "You can't miss it," would take on hilarious meaning for me during the next three years as I drove miles of western Oklahoma roads, looking for the homes of the wonderful women who would become my consultants for this collection of Cheyenne women's songs. It is indeed possible to miss "it," and I did get lost on many occasions. But although the physical sense of direction on the highways and backroads was often misleading, my sense of being on the right track while working on this project has never faltered.

My first steps into American Indian music took place when David McAllester introduced me to its beauty at the Music in General Studies Institute of the College Music Society, held in Boulder in 1988. After leaving those mountaintops of Colorado and returning to the flatlands of Oklahoma, I listened, almost continually, to music of Plains tribes on records and cassettes. Occasional visits to powwows made me hungry to know more; I heard complex music vigorously performed, and I watched the extraordinary giveaways of useful and beautiful things. Who were these people, I wondered, these people who give so generously, make such good jokes, and have so much pride in who they are? I didn't want to know only about the music, I wanted to know the people.

So when I stepped into the Hawk household and met Diane, I was eager to learn about Oklahoma Indian family life as well as music. I didn't know that I was meeting the woman who would become my best friend and my Cheyenne sister, who would share her family and home with me, who would joke and laugh and cry with me at the sun dance, who would teach me to make frybread under a willow shade in the hot June wind, who would ask me to help coach her daughter Consuelo during the advent of the first Hawk grandchild, who would sit quietly in my house and support me with her prayers while I sweated out the last chapters of my dissertation.

The choice of subject for that dissertation—the basis of this book—was an answer to a prayer at the 1990 Southern Cheyenne Sun Dance. During a solemn time of prayer and giving, Diane took my offering of fabric to the pile of cloth to be placed in the fork of the center pole of the sun dance arbor. My contribution to Thunder's Nest commemorated my desire to devote careful research to some aspect of Cheyenne music—music that I had grown to love so much from the people that I had grown to respect so highly. Knowing that music is holy ground to Cheyenne people, I wanted to be sure that my research questions would be an appropriate inquiry from an outsider.

On the way back from the ceremony to my home in Norman, the plan began to take shape. I wondered about music that was not for ceremony, music of everyday life—life away from the sun dance. Had everyday songs ever existed among Cheyenne people, and did anyone remember them or use them now? I wondered whether Cheyenne people sang songs while they worked or played or visited. Did Cheyenne songs exist that could be sung by anyone, anytime, anywhere? What kinds of songs were there, what did they sound like, how did they come to be sung?

There is a saying common among American Indian people in Oklahoma: "If you want to know something, ask a woman." I decided to follow this advice and seek consultants among Cheyenne women to determine the answers to my questions. Diane Hawk passed the word among her friends and relatives, and she and her daughter Consuelo accompanied me on visits to their houses and workplaces. Sometimes I went by myself, carrying with me a letter of introduction from Diane, who is in charge of tribal enrollment for the Cheyenne and Arapaho tribes of Oklahoma.

I also traveled with a copy of Frances Densmore's *Cheyenne and Arapaho Music,* in which I read about her visit to Oklahoma in 1935 to collect, transcribe, and analyze Indian music. It was an eerie moment when I first opened Densmore's book and found the photograph of her primary consultant, Bob-Tail Wolf, whose home he had offered as a base for her recording and interviewing. My sister Diane Hawk is Bob-Tail Wolf's great-great-granddaughter.[1]

Meeting Diane and her family was the beginning of this book, and the beginning of other valued friendships among

---

1. Although Frances Densmore refers to Diane's relative as Bob-Tailed Wolf, Diane informs me (in both her office as keeper of tribal records and as great-great-granddaughter) that the man was always known as Bob-Tail Wolf. Therefore, this spelling will be used in this book.

Oklahoma Cheyenne people. Their generosity has had a profound effect on my life; I have learned much about hospitality,
sharing, and tolerance. I have also learned new definitions of
courage and patience. With gratitude I acknowledge my family
of cultural consultants: the Burton Hawks, Elouise Swallow and
her daughters, and Grandma Nellie Roman Nose. My friends
and singer/consultants Bertha Little Coyote, Mary Fletcher Armstrong, Rena Buffalo Meat Young Bear, Mary Lou Birdshead
Blackbear, Rhoda Young Bird Braxton, Wilma Blackowl Hamilton, Imogene Jones, Mary Lou Stone Road Prairie Chief, Joan
Swallow, and June Warden Black were gracious and informa-
tive, and the personal inspiration I gained from their stories
continues to influence my thinking and my listening.

For her expertise in writing and translating Cheyenne, I am
indebted to Lenora Hart, whose good humor and patience
lasted through hours of painstaking transcription of recorded
song texts. The maps were the precise work of cartographer
Sue Kahre-Stradford. Judith Gray, ethnomusicologist for the
Federal Cylinder Project, American Folk Life Center of the
Library of Congress, provided essential advice and contributed
her expertise in transcription of American Indian musics.

The illustrations of hand-game materials and signals were
the work of Paul Corrigan, a University of Oklahoma graduate
student, who entered into this "labor of love" (as he called it)
with much imagination. For their photographic skills I am
indebted to Dr. Mary Jo Ruggles and J. Pat Carter. Postproduc-
tion of the field tape was the work of Barry Stramp, and for his
special sensitivity I am grateful. Thanks also are due to Donald
De Witt, John Lovett, and the staff of the Western History
Collections of the University of Oklahoma for their support
and assistance.

John Drayton, Kim Wiar, Sarah Morrison, and the staff at
the University of Oklahoma Press were unfailingly considerate

and took time to teach me a great deal about writing. Mary Jo Ruggles, my colleague and friend, helped in many ways: my family and I will always be grateful for her caring and kindness. Finally, I thank David McAllester for the blessing of his many years of experience, his helpful suggestions, his listening ear, his tolerance for my noisy enthusiasm, his belief in the importance of the project, his trust in my ability, and his spirituality that enabled him to comprehend what this project meant to me.

Southern Cheyenne Women's Songs

Introduction

It is easy to forget that Cheyenne women are ordinary, everyday people. The mystique that surrounds "Indian-ness," a residue of the popular images supplied by Hollywood and romantic novels, can keep us from seeing that Oklahoma Cheyenne people function in the mainstream modern world: going to work, getting the children to school, attending church, voting, watching television. But in addition to typical American activities, many Oklahoma Cheyenne people continue to participate in traditional activities that make them unique. Essential information about that uniqueness can be learned by listening to the voices of Cheyenne women, voices that in the past have often gone unheard.

Part of the special power of Cheyenne women's music is its communal purpose, perpetuating and affirming the culture's traditions through song, dance, and ceremony. The music is also intensely personal, bringing individuals close to God, to family, and to the memories and spirits of departed loved ones. Rooted in traditional ways, Cheyenne women are also modern Americans whose music is influenced by styles accessible by means of current technology. Musical innovations take place as traditional styles evolve and contemporary ideas are added.

Very little field recording of Oklahoma Cheyenne women's music has been done. The first significant study of Cheyenne traditional song types was Frances Densmore's monograph *Cheyenne and Arapaho Music* (1936), based on field recordings made at the home of Bob-Tail Wolf in Kingfisher, Oklahoma, a small town north and west of Oklahoma City. Densmore brought to her investigation a mind-set rooted in the Western European tradition of notated music; her analyses were concerned with melodic material and tone systems. Although Densmore's study documented several songs sung by women, only paraphrased translations were presented; no text underlay accompanied the musical transcriptions. Densmore's focus was music of the past, and like many scholars of her generation, she was motivated by the desire to preserve music that was feared to be in danger of extinction.

This book recognizes that Oklahoma Cheyenne music is far from extinct, and that the old music lives on and new music is developing. In describing Cheyenne music, the words "traditional" and "contemporary" are not mutually exclusive. The handed-down-from-the-past lives side by side with the new and fresh, and performers are influenced by phenomena from both inside and outside the culture. For example, an old lullaby cannot be perceived by a child who also listens to rock music the same way it was by a child fifty years ago. At the same time, a traditional Cheyenne data base (acquired by virtue of birth within the culture) might be required to understand the depth of meaning in a new spiritual song sung with contemporary Euro-American harmonic accompaniment. Contemporary music does not exclude the past, nor does tradition cease in the light of contemporary innovation.

These principles make it clear that context information—that is, information from Cheyennes about where, when, why, and by whom a song would be sung—is vitally important to a complete musical understanding. Without the stories of the people involved, how can anyone appreciate the value of a song or get any sense of its efficacy within the culture? Therefore, this book contains as much context information as it was possible to ascertain, with mythological references explored and historical sources consulted in order to formulate the most complete mosaic of data.

The song analyses in this book include the Cheyenne point of view as expressed in the comments of the musicians themselves. It also includes my own Euro-American aesthetic analysis; it would be foolish to pretend that I don't put my own tile in the data mosaic. I have also included the thoughts of Densmore and other twentieth-century students of Native American music and culture. Since the Cheyennes have no indigenous music notation system, I have transcribed the songs into standard Western notation. Because some nuances of Indian songs have no traditional Western symbols, it was necessary to make adjustments in standard notation in order to accommodate Cheyenne musical qualities.

In addition to analysis of musical content, there is an emphasis on texts in this song collection. Song texts were translated by Lenora Hart, education director for the Cheyenne-Arapaho Tribes of Oklahama, and written in a locally accepted Southern Cheyenne orthography. Following McAllester's paradigm, translations consist of four parts: (1) translation of song text into ordinary spoken Cheyenne, (2) song text reflecting any changes between spoken language and song text, (3) word-for-word translation, and (4) free translation to make the meaning clearer to English speakers.

The women who sang the songs for this project are enrolled members of the Southern Cheyenne and Arapaho tribes. Several of the consultants for this project are both Cheyenne and Arapaho in heritage. Although the two tribes differ in many traditional religious and cultural aspects, there are intermarriages between the tribes. Since 1851 the U.S. government has recognized the southern branches of both the Cheyenne and Arapaho tribes as one entity. The southern and northern divisions of the Cheyenne tribe are separated in location and are independent in tribal business matters. The Northern Cheyenne Tribe lives in Montana, where an intact reservation still exists. The Oklahoma Cheyenne and Arapaho reservation lands were allotted in severalty as a result of the Dawes Act of 1887. Not all enrollees in the southern Cheyenne and Arapaho tribes live in Oklahoma, although the majority of them do. All of the women who sang for this book live in Oklahoma.

The Cheyennes place high value on music. Music's power as a spiritual force is well known to American Indians, and many songs are restricted as to who can perform or even have an opportunity to listen to them. Music that is traditionally the domain of Cheyenne men is incidental to this book's purpose, which is to bring to light the contribution of women to the music culture of the Cheyenne people. Music is considered to be a gift from a spiritual source, and to sing a song for another is a gift to the listener. Songs of personal spirituality were recorded and transcribed only by request of the singer; no music of a secret or private ceremonial nature was recorded or transcribed.

Chapter One

Cheyenne Culture and History

CHEYENNE MUSIC, TRADITIONS, AND CEREMONY

Cheyenne music is born with a purpose, and Cheyenne song, like Cheyenne ceremony, is not treated lightly. Ceremonial music of the Cheyennes accompanies profound and intense traditional worship. But everyday life is also considered a ritual occasion. Cheyenne Headman Burton Hawk says, "Cheyennes don't do nothing without a ceremony. For us, everything has to have a ceremony—everything."

Most academic historical accounts of the Cheyennes leave out this aspect of Cheyenne life, centering instead on events concerning the tribe's relations with the U.S. government since the eighteenth century. To balance this view, it is necessary to become acquainted with Cheyenne culture; only then can we begin to see the impact and ramifications of historical events on the Cheyenne people themselves, people who are quintessentially spiritually motivated.

Cheyenne culture is rooted in religious beliefs concerning the holy man, Sweet Medicine, and his visions within the sacred mountain Na ko vo sso (Bear Butte), just east of the Black Hills in South Dakota. Sweet Medicine's revelations within the mountain established the charter, laws, tribal circle, religion, and mobile way of life of the people. In a spiritual encounter, Sweet Medicine received four Sacred Arrows and a holy code of laws

from Ma hi yo, the creator god. These laws are the root of a traditional legal system that handled complex problems efficiently.

In addition to the Sacred Arrows, the Cheyenne Buffalo Hat,
a two-horned headpiece (once a relic of the Sutaio tribe's religion), was incorporated into Cheyenne rituals (just as the
Sutaio themselves were incorporated as a band within the
Cheyennes). Observance of the rituals of the Sacred Arrows
and the Buffalo Hat, along with the annual sun dance ceremonies, remain the central traditional religious expressions of the
Cheyennes to this day.

The elaborate ceremonies for renewal of the Sacred Arrows
and the southern sun dance are held in Oklahoma every summer near the end of June. The Arrow ceremony precedes the
sun dance, and the two are considered necessary for the puri-
fication of and renewal of blessings for the world. At a contemporary sun dance, men and women undertake an ordeal of
fasting from food and water and endurance of summer heat for
seventy-two hours as they devote themselves to intense prayer
for their families, the tribe, and the good of the world. The
men dance on piles of sweet-smelling sage in a smoky arbor
made of trees and willow branches, blowing eagle bone whis-
tles with each beat of the drum. The female participants re-
cline within the arbor, are painted and instructed, and lend
spiritual support to the men while engaging in their own physical hardships and spiritual experience.

Camping at the sun dance ceremonies is an annual event for
Oklahoma Cheyenne traditionalist families; here they live together in a way that brings back to them the feeling of the past.
The ceremonies are not open to the public, and photography
and audio recording are not permitted except under special
circumstances. Tipis are used by families lucky enough to af-
ford them, and regular tents and sometimes vans can be found
in the camping circle. Food for the ceremonies is cooked over

open fires; old customs concerning the handling of food, water, camping tools, and fire tending are strictly followed. During the sun dance, supporting family members sit around the arbor to lend their spiritual strength to the dancers during their ordeal; the dance is a place of blessing to both active participants and supporting family and friends.

Not all Cheyennes subscribe solely to the traditional ceremonial religion. Many incorporate other beliefs into their religious activities. There are devout Cheyenne members of the Native American Church, a religion involving the use of peyote in night-long ceremonies; an entire repertoire of peyote songs enhances this form of religious expression. The Native American Church crosses tribal boundaries and is a nationwide phenomenon. Other Cheyennes belong to various Christian faiths, including Roman Catholic, Baptist, Methodist, Mennonite, and Pentecostal churches. Some Christian Cheyennes have repudiated traditional tribal religion altogether and adhere strictly to the tenets of their chosen sect. In all of these various religious expressions, the performance and composition of Christian devotional songs are common practices in present-day Oklahoma. Devout Cheyennes of all sects often worship through original, recently composed music that uses Cheyenne as well as English texts.

A significant collection of Cheyenne hymnody has been notated under the auspices of the Mennonite Church. Hymns from collections first initiated by the missionary Rodolphe Petter in 1907 have been compiled along with newer compositions into the hymnal *Tsese-Ma'heone-Nemeotòtse*. The written Cheyenne text underlay for the hymns is based on recent linguistic work among the Northern Cheyennes in Montana.[1]

---

1. Graber, *Tsese-Ma'heone-Nemeotòtse: Cheyenne Spiritual Songs.*

This hymnal is not in common use in Oklahoma due to the differences in writing systems among the northern and southern branches of the tribe. Instead, Southern Cheyennes rely on the traditional method of oral and aural transmission of songs.

Although modes of writing the language differ, Cheyenne speakers from both the northern and southern branches understand each other. The two branches of the tribe are separated geographically, but that separation has not altered the feeling of the people that they are one tribe. The yearly gathering to renew the Sacred Arrows in the south has its counterpart in the Buffalo Hat ceremony in the north; visitors from both branches may visit each ceremony. Sun dance ceremonies are celebrated in both the north and the south; if conditions preclude the sun dance in one area, all participants gather in the other area for a unified celebration.

Whether Northern or Southern, Cheyennes value close and extended family ties. The Cheyenne concept of family is extensive, with blood ties binding even distant relatives. Historically and currently, Cheyenne children are often coparented by various relatives. Cheyenne kinship terms do not correspond to standard English dictionary terminology. Children have many mothers and grandmothers in the form of aunts and great aunts; various female kin are frequently addressed as "Mom," "Auntie," or "Grandma" depending on generation. Uncles are "fathers," and cousins are considered to be "brothers" and "sisters." In the life of a Cheyenne child, correction, advice, and affection are received from a variety of relatives; respect for the elderly is characteristic of the Cheyenne people.[2]

At present as well as in the past, intermarriages between

2. For an extensive discussion of Cheyenne kinship, see Moore, *Cheyenne Nation*.

Cheyennes and non-Cheyennes are common; marriages be-tween Cheyennes and Arapahos in Oklahoma are particularly frequent. Even in past centuries there has been intermarriage between the Cheyennes and members of other tribes, African-Americans, and Caucasians. One notable marriage between a white man and a Cheyenne woman took place in 1835 be-tween the trader William Bent and Owl Woman, the daughter of White Thunder, the keeper of the Sacred Arrows. Their union resulted in a family line that continues to have annual reunion dances and powwows in Oklahoma. Today, marriages between Oklahoma Cheyennes and whites are not uncommon.

Both in marriage and in other social roles, today's Cheyenne women lead lives as diverse as any others in the female Ameri-can population. Historically, Cheyenne women were noted for their dignity and chastity, and wielded strong moral influence within the tribe. George Bird Grinnell, who wrote at length concerning his observations of Cheyenne life of the late nine-teenth and early twentieth centuries, comments:

> Among the Cheyennes, the women have great influence. They discuss matters freely with their husbands, argue over points, persuade, cajole, and usually have their own way about tribal matters. They are, in fact, the final authority in the camp. There are traditions of women chiefs and of women who have pos-sessed remarkable mysterious powers or have shown great wis-dom in council. If in later days the women did not take part in councils, they nevertheless exercised on the men of their fami-lies an influence that can hardly be overestimated, and in the councils so frequently held, where only men spoke, this influ-ence of the women was always felt. (1923, 156–57)

Nineteenth-century economic changes left Cheyenne women disadvantaged within the tribe. When the buffalo robe trade was at its peak, Plains women found themselves in the middle of a male-dominated system that controlled the acquisition and trade of the robes women processed. Bea Medicine observes that "growing economic dependency" made Plains women "more vulnerable to the interests and machinations of men," and the desire to act in ways that were "independent and decisive," yet still socially acceptable, led to variations on the "typical" female role among tribes (269, 273). A major Cheyenne variation was the institution of warrior women, who played important roles both on the battlefield and in preparation for war and homecomings.

Historical reports document the exploits of valiant warrior women during the nineteenth-century battles against U.S. soldiers. The most frequently mentioned is Calf Road Woman, who rode to battle armed with a six-shooter in the company of her brother Comes in Sight. When her brother's horse was shot under him, Calf Road Woman charged the enemy, pulled her brother onto her horse, and rode away to safety. Among the Cheyennes, this battle (which occurred on the Rosebud River in Montana) became known as "Where the Girl Saved Her Brother."

Not only did women on occasion join men in war, but they also played an important role in supporting and encouraging warriors. An example is the singing of "wolf songs" before battle; warrior scouts were known as "wolves." Wolf songs were sung between sweethearts before war parted them from each other; these are sometimes known as "war journey songs," serving to sustain memories of important relationships during the stress of war. Another kind of war song inspired bravery, sometimes with texts that could be personalized by including an individual's name. These war-related songs demonstrate women's use of music as a powerful influence to honor and encourage those who they believed were making sacrifices for the good of the tribe.

At the warriors' return, ceremonies took place as an expression of thanksgiving for their safety and to commemorate brave exploits. One type of ceremonial dance in which women had an important role was the scalp dance. Grinnell describes the events of these extended ceremonies as they were held in the nineteenth century, including ceremonial feasting, body painting, dancing, socializing, and song.

A World War I scalp dance ceremony was described in the *Watonga* (Oklahoma) *Republican* in 1918. The event included a parade of men and women singing "old time war songs," with the women dangling imitation scalps on poles "to imitate the blood of the scalped Hun."[3] This dramatic description illustrates the impact of such events on both the Indian and non-Indian community in the early twentieth century. As the twenty-first century nears, Cheyenne soldier homecoming celebrations can still be found, as in the case of the Ed Wilson family, who prepared a traditional welcome when their son returned from a tour of Saudi Arabia in 1991.[4] In the Cheyenne community today, such ceremonies also take place to honor servicewomen.

The soldier homecoming celebrations of the 1990s demonstrate that the custom still retains its traditional function; other events take place outside the community to strengthen those traditions by means of teaching and demonstration. For example, a group of Cheyenne and Arapaho women demonstrated a traditional scalp dance for the Oklahoma Institute of Indian Heritage's 1990 Fall Fest Exhibition in Oklahoma City. Active veterans' dancing societies, their auxiliaries, and women's so-

---

3. Darrell Rice, ed. and comp., *Their Story: A Pioneer Days Album of the Blaine County Area*, 20–21. The "scalps" used in the parade were made of black-haired dog skins attached to red flannel.

4. Burton, "Norman Man Plans Tribal Ceremony for Warrior Son," *Normal* (Okla.) *Transcript*, April 14, 1991, p. 1 (A).

cieties known as "War Mothers Clubs" travel throughout the state and dance at powwows and social dances called "benefits."

Benefit dances are held to raise money for special purposes. For example, an elder grandparent or friend might sponsor a dance for a young person who is leaving home and family to attend college or join the armed forces. A service group, such as an education committee, might sponsor a dance to raise funds for a particular cause, such as the purchase of school supplies for needy students. Similar dances are held for family reunions or to raise funds for family needs. These dances are occasions of visiting, dancing, and being together with family and tribal members. Another dance event that is similar in format to the benefit dance is the memorial dance, held in honor of a deceased person by the family. Special memorial songs are sung and rituals enacted to heal the grief of the survivors of the deceased. Along with these ceremonies, a dinner is held, and social dances are enjoyed.

Of the social dance forms one might observe at a benefit dance, the most common are war dances, round dances, and gourd dances. Street clothes are the common attire for benefit dances, supplemented with triangular fringed shawls for women and long, rectangular "gourd dance shawls" for men. The gourd dance is so named after the gourd shakers held by the men as they dance in place, stepping in place with the beat of the drum. Gourd dances come in sets of four, and women in fringed shawls dance behind the male dancers in an attitude known as "backing them up" or "supporting." The war dance is like a stately walk, with all dancers circling the drum with erect posture, one step per beat. Round dancing is more casual, although quite dignified; it is a circular side-stepping dance of quicker pace. In all these dances, straight posture and grace define the aesthetic.

Benefit dances often last through the afternoon and into the early hours of the morning. It is easy to get tired at such a long event, but the music supplies the participants with energy. After one particularly vigorous set of gourd dances, a middle-aged woman resumed her seat with a happy sigh, commenting, "That was a good one." A teen-age girl asked her, "What do you mean by a good one, Auntie? I always hear people talk about good, but I don't hear what you mean." Her aunt replied, "Well, it's like when everybody's real tired, and doesn't feel like dancing, but they get on up and do it, and then the drum sounds real good, and makes you want to dance, and you feel like dancing real good. That's a good one—it's a feeling everybody gets."

Another factor in good feelings gained at benefit dances has to do with "giveaways," demonstrations of generosity, gratitude, and respect involving the formal presentation of gifts. Baskets of groceries, blankets, household items, shawls, and other beautiful or useful gifts are presented; ceremonial procedures demonstrate an exchange of respect and appreciation between giver and receiver. Frequent informal giftgiving is a part of everyday life among Cheyenne people; Cheyenne ritual giveaways permeate both religious observances and social events. Hundreds of dollars worth of gifts are given and received at benefit dances.

Another type of social dance is the Forty-Nine, which in its present-day form has a questionable reputation among Cheyenne elders. In the nineteenth-century prototype, dances were held late at night when, at the invitation of elders, young people gathered for socializing and singing. Wolf songs, war journey songs, and songs from other tribes evolved into the Forty-Nine repertoire. The traditional activity has waxed and waned; the intervention of two world wars has had the effect of intermittent revival of the custom, because Forty-Nines were held in honor of departing soldiers. The nocturnal Forty-Nine is now an American pan-Indian phenomenon. English words, vocables, and native-language phrases combine to form the texts of many Forty-Nine songs; the song form is simple and the texts are pithy and often humorously suggestive. The accompanying movement is a round-dance step, with dancers locking arms in a circle around the drum. Elders consulted for this project have mixed viewpoints on the Forty-Nine, but most agree that it has departed from its intended social purpose and has degenerated into a scene of too much drinking and pugnacious behavior. (Possible origins of the Forty-Nine are discussed in chapter 5.) The popular Forty-Nine song repertoire is enjoyed by many Cheyennes through the medium of commercial cassette tapes.

In addition to singing and dancing events, Cheyenne people have traditional games that continue to provide entertainment at present-day activities. One such game that enjoys great popularity in Oklahoma is the hand game, a form of amusement accompanied by a song repertoire of its own. The game involves the use of two bone beads, one of them marked; two teams of individuals compete to guess the hand hiding the marked bead. Good humor permeates a hand game event; in the hand game as well as in other aspects of life, the Cheyennes value laughter and jokes. The lively, quick-paced game songs are accompanied by small hand-held drums.

The drum is the heart of any Cheyenne musical activity. Drums differ in size and construction according to function and context. Hand game drums are usually one-sided frame drums. They are small enough to be supported vertically in a man's lap with one arm while the opposite hand wields a drumstick. Forty-Nine drums are made of wood and hide and have handles that make it possible for several people to suspend the drum while standing around it; this drum shares the communal characteristic of its context. Peyote drums are made of iron kettles, containing a small quantity of water, over which a hide is stretched and tied. These were used historically in religious observances involving hallucinogenic cactus, now incorporated into contemporary Native American Church ritual.

A large two-headed drum, occasionally suspended on a four-staked frame, is used at the sun dance, powwows, and benefit dances. The instrument is sometimes called a powwow drum, and the instrument is created with reverent preparation and sacred purpose. The beating sticks are long, allowing room for eight to twelve seated men to encircle the drum and play at the same time. In this context, the term "drum" is expanded to mean both the instrument and the group of players and singers. Women also sing with the drum, sitting in a circle behind the men. Gifts are regularly presented to the drum at ceremonials and dances; the drum returns thanks by means of a vigorous drumroll.

The pounding of the powwow drum accompanies the event most familiar to non-Cheyennes. ("Powwow" was originally an Algonquian term for "conjurer".) These events were held originally for the purpose of curing diseases, ensuring success in battle, or bringing good hunting. Oklahoma Cheyenne pow-wows occur in the summer months in outdoor settings. Two to three days in length, powwows usually involve dance competitions. Families from many tribes come to camp and visit, and non-Indian visitors are welcomed. A highlight of the powwow is the evening "grand entry," a drum-centered circular parade that can involve a hundred or more dancers of all ages in flamboyant regalia. From "tiny tots" to "golden age" dancers, male and female participants compete for cash awards in several dance categories: ladies' fancy shawl, buckskin, cloth, and jingle dress dances; and men's straight, traditional, grass, and fancy dances.

There is an observable music education process at powwows as boys are allowed to join the elders at the drum and young girls sit with the women backup singers (the "chorus"). Giveaways commemorate musical "firsts," such as a child entering the dance arena for the first time or when a young man is first invited to be the head singer. "Tiny tots" and "junior" divisions at competition dances are other examples that demonstrate the Cheyenne community's concern that children learn to perform and respond to music at an early age.

Cheyenne families also travel to powwows held by other tribes and compete in large competition events such as Oklahoma City's annual Red Earth Festival and the Oklahoma Institute of Indian Heritage's Fall Fest. Although the spiritual or aesthetic roots of the various styles of powwow dancing may or may not be Cheyenne, many participate in this intertribal activity while retaining their Cheyenne identity.

Another popular recreational activity for today's Oklahoma Cheyennes, both men and women, is the game of bingo. The Southern Cheyenne and Arapaho Tribal Complex at Concho provides a building for Concho Bingo. This tribal industry attracts people from miles around to the bingo hall to try their luck; Indians from other tribes, whites, Hispanics, and blacks sit together in a friendly atmosphere for hours. Hundreds of dollars are won and are viewed by many as a much-needed income supplement.

Modern bingo enterprises sell packs of large tear-off sheets with nine or more colorful bingo cards printed on each newsprint-thin page. Rather than using bean or button markers of old-fashioned bingo, players now use "dabbers," sponge-tipped devices designed to stamp a circle of translucent ink on the bingo numbers. Dabbers, also called "dobbers," are available in a variety of ink colors, including fluorescent oranges, pinks, and yellows.

Most Cheyenne events have a musical repertoire, that is, a

catalog of songs that are an integral part of the activity. Bingo, however, owing to the concentration required for playing, does not have a song repertoire. Instead, the "music" of the game lies in the caller's litany and the chance rhythmic surprises of the winners' exclamations. Callers have varying styles of intoning the numbers, and the aesthetic of bingo calling involves clarity, accuracy, uniformity of tempo, and pleasant tone quality. Like the "music" of tobacco auctioneers or the cries of street vendors, bingo calling is an art that many would not consider music. But the fact that the sound of a good bingo caller can be described and is appreciated shows that this aural phenomenon takes its place within the repertoire of Cheyenne sound.

Not only is bingo an aural event, but it can also be an opportunity to see traditional art in a functional setting. Cheyenne beadwork enters the bingo hall in the form of beaded bingo dabbers, and some bingo enthusiasts who also do beadwork bring their wares along for informal show and sale among friends. "Happiness is playing bingo" shirts are a common sight. Bingo jokes are told by masters of ceremonies at powwows; the camp crier at the 1989 sun dance amused the sweating crowd by announcing, "The Bingo Bus will be leaving in five minutes!" Like the hand game, the powwow, and the benefit dance, bingo now plays an important role in social and cultural cohesion.

The people of the Southern Cheyenne tribe continue to live unobtrusively among the citizens of the state's majority culture. Often not fitting entirely into the mold of white society, Cheyennes continue to persevere as a people in spite of political and economic setbacks. Patriotism and loyalty both to tribe and country are demonstrated enthusiastically in song, ceremony, and service in the armed forces. Generosity, good humor, hospitality, and love for family are characteristic. Cheyenne spiritual life is rich in its various forms; artistic expression is highly prized, and all types of music are valued and respected by the people.

SKETCH OF HISTORICAL EVENTS

Hospitality marked the Cheyennes' first documented contact with Europeans in 1680, when a party of Cheyennes visited La Salle's Fort Crèvecoeur on the Illinois River and invited the fur traders to visit their village area up the Mississippi. Having migrated from their aboriginal area in eastern Canada, the Cheyennes settled in agricultural villages in Minnesota. From villages in the Great Lakes and Upper Mississippi region, they moved around 1700 into the Dakota Black Hills, the region of Na ko vo sso, the sacred mountain. By 1740 the Cheyennes had acquired large herds of horses, and in the Black Hills the Cheyennes grew crops in a system of "untended horticulture"; in summer the people left their planted fields and moved their horses to the grasslands, returning to harvest in the fall and spend the winter in the Black Hills (Moore, 140–41). This system allowed the tribe to conserve their home firewood supply, gather summer wild-growing foods as insurance against crop failure, and graze their horses on the abundant prairie grasses.

When the horse herds outgrew their winter grass supplies, the Cheyennes moved farther south and west into the grasslands of the plains. As the Cheyennes searched for the essentials of water to drink, grass for their horses, and wood for their fires, they roamed from place to place and were noted for their skill with horses. In the plains they hunted buffalo, which provided food as well as clothing (buffalo robes) and shelter (skin coverings for tipis).

In the early 1800s Lewis and Clark found the Cheyennes to be the most populous tribe in the Black Hills. The main group then lived in the vicinity of the Missouri River, and during this

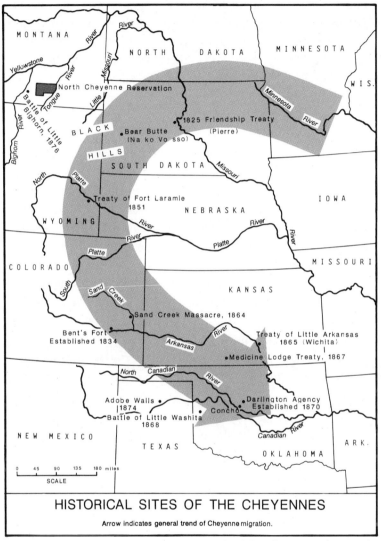

HISTORICAL SITES OF THE CHEYENNES

Arrow indicates general trend of Cheyenne migration.

Adapted from Stan Hoig, *The Peace Chiefs of the Cheyennes* (University of Oklahoma Press, 1980).

time they became hunting allies and neighbors with the smaller Sutaio tribe. The Sutaio and Cheyenne, both of Algonquian linguistic stock, found themselves able to communicate with each other. The Buffalo Hat of the Sutaio was incorporated into the religion of the Cheyennes, and the Sutaio were later formally united with the Cheyenne tribe as a distinct band.

A treaty made with the United States in 1825 marks the beginning of a period of complex and often tragic relations with white people. At the head of the Teton River (near present-day Pierre, South Dakota), the Cheyenne and Sioux held a council with U.S. Army officers who were sent to make treaties with the tribes for the purpose of protection of the fur trade, which had grown as a result of the Lewis and Clark expedition. After a display of rocketry and howitzer shell explosions performed by the military brigade, the Cheyennes were persuaded to sign the first "friendship" treaty, acknowledging the right of the U.S. government to regulate all trade. Fur traders introduced whiskey to the Cheyennes, a regrettable circumstance that brought much grief to the people.

Other major changes were brought about by the trade of buffalo robes. John H. Moore writes:

> Because the robes embodied a huge amount of women's work, polygynous families grew up that were organized around a group of co-wives who were also co-workers and sisters to one another. . . . families were reorganized to accommodate the demands of robe making. . . . Because of trade, by 1850 the Cheyennes had transformed themselves from a marginal horticultural tribe of the Middle Missouri to a very successful nation of hunters and traders. (138)

The buffalo robe business effected a major event in the relocation and settlement of southern bands of Cheyennes. In 1824 Charles and William Bent and Céran St. Vrain built a stockade at the mouth of the Fountain River (the site of present-

day Pueblo, Colorado) as a base for beaver trapping. Trade
with the Indians developed, and the Cheyenne chief Yellow
Wolf advised the Bents to build a more convenient trading
post on the Arkansas River, thus bringing about the establishment of Bent's Fort in 1834 (near present day La Junta, about a
hundred miles southeast of Colorado Springs). Buffalo robes
were prepared by Cheyenne women and traded by the men,
and by the 1840s the Bent and St. Vrain Company was a thriv-
ing fur business second in America only to the John Jacob
Astor's company. While a remnant of the tribe continued the
old nomadic way of life, roaming the headwaters of the North
Platte and Yellowstone rivers, the main body of the Cheyennes
moved to the Bent's Fort area. William Bent's marriage in 1835
to Owl Woman reinforced friendly relations between Bent's
Fort and the southern Cheyenne bands who settled in the area.

Another tribe that traded with the Bents was the Arapahos,
who had been Cheyenne allies in hunting and battle since the
late eighteenth century and possibly before. Both from Algonquian linguistic stock, their relationship had been mutually
beneficial even from its earliest stages in the eighteenth century. After decades of warfare pitted the Cheyenne and Arapaho tribes against Kiowas, Comanches, and Plains Apaches,
the five tribes met for a peace council at Bent's Fort in 1840.

The Cheyennes located around Bent's Fort became part of
the division of the tribe officially known as the Southern Cheyennes in 1851. The Cheyennes, Arapahos, and Brulé Sioux
were distressed about the influx of whites into their lands,
bringing diseases such as cholera and smallpox and destroy-
ing the buffalo ranges. Some compensation was promised by
the U.S. government in the Treaty of Fort Laramie in 1851. In
addition, the government sought to define a reserved territory
in which each tribe could live and hunt; this was the beginning
of the reservation system for the Cheyennes.

In utter ignorance and disregard of the Cheyenne system of dealing with social problems, the government ordered the tribe to choose a single representative to exercise control and be responsible for the actions of the whole tribe. As compensation for the disruption of the buffalo environment, the government representative promised fifty thousand dollars' worth of goods per year for fifty years. In exchange, the Indians were to allow whites safe travel through their lands and give the U.S. government the right to build military posts. This treaty was a very serious matter to the Cheyennes, carried out in the presence of all the Chiefs, and sealed with a Sacred Arrow ceremony.

The Southern Cheyennes and Arapahos were assigned lands in present-day southeastern Wyoming, northeastern Colorado, southwestern Nebraska, and northwestern Kansas—approximately 122,000 square miles). Eight months later, Congress sent back a revised treaty that reduced their annuities from fifty years to ten; several chiefs signed it. At the time of the Fort Laramie treaty, the Southern Cheyennes were unaware that their important role in the economy of the American West was waning.

By 1860 new economic interests occupied white entrepreneurs of the West: farming, ranching, and mining. Tales of abundant mineral wealth drew settlers and prospectors, and the rush to the land brought in its wake Indian resistance to encroachments on their territory. Growing hysteria among threatened pioneers and Denver entrepreneurs set the stage for the Sand Creek Massacre.

At dawn on November 28, 1864. Col. John Chivington led an unprovoked attack on a group of Cheyennes and Arapahos camped at Sand Creek. Although Chief Black Kettle waved both American and white flags to show the peaceful nature of the camp, he was forced to witness the atrocious genocide: two hundred people killed, most of whom were women and

CHEYENNE LANDS BY VARIOUS TREATIES

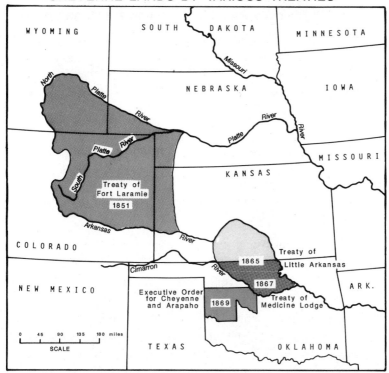

Adapted from Donald J. Berthrong, *The Southern Cheyennes* (University of Oklahoma Press, 1963).

children. His wife was shot nine times, but survived. The bodies of the slain were mutilated, most of them beyond recognition. The troops returned to Denver and, with the full approbation of their commanding officer, displayed scalps and other grisly souvenirs of their victory.

The Sand Creek Massacre was investigated by a joint committee of both houses of Congress in 1865, and the subsequent report contained the opinion that Indian wars could be traced to lawless white aggression. Concerning Chivington, the report of the Joint Committee on the Conduct of the War stated:

> Your committee can hardly find fitting terms to describe his conduct. . . . he deliberately planned and executed a foul and dastardly massacre. . . . Having full knowledge of their friendly character, having himself been instrumental to some extent in placing them in their position of fancied security, he took advantage of their inapprehension and defenceless condition to gratify the worst passions that ever cursed the heart of man. . . . Your committee most sincerely trust that the result of their inquiry will be the adoption of measures which will render impossible the employment of officers . . . such as have heretofore made the administration of Indian affairs in this country a byword and reproach.[5]

The government promised reparations to the Cheyennes; to this day, compensatory emoluments have not been made in full to Sand Creek survivors and descendants.

Although Black Kettle and his followers continued to work for peace with the whites after Sand Creek, many Cheyennes previously friendly to the whites became eager for vengeance and prepared to attack overland stage routes. Hostilities between Plains tribes and the whites prompted an attempt at a truce and a meeting of the Cheyennes and Arapahos with government officials in 1865 on the Arkansas River (at the site of present-day Wichita).

A new reservation was proposed for the tribes, relocating the people from the buffalo lands through which the stage was routed to an area south of the Arkansas River. The new reservation would occupy approximately thirty thousand square miles in south central Kansas and north central Oklahoma—

5. U.S. Congress, Joint Committee on the Conduct of the War, *Massacre of Cheyenne Indians,* 38th Cong., 2d sess., 1865, S. Rept. 142, 7–8.

less than one-third of the more than 122,000 square miles promised by the Fort Laramie Treaty of 1851. Before signing the treaty, Chief Black Kettle stated: "Your young soldiers, I don't think they listen to you. You bring presents, and when I come to get them I am afraid they will strike me before I get away. When I come in to receive presents I take them up crying" (Berthrong 1963, 242). Some Cheyenne chiefs expressed concern that those not present at the meeting might not be inclined to move away from their lands. Still, they promised to do what they could to promote peaceful relations between the tribe and the whites. Signing the Treaty of Little Arkansas in 1865, the Cheyennes ceded all of their previously claimed lands, retaining only the rights to the range unoccupied by white settlers between the Arkansas and Platte rivers.

Young Cheyennes raided farms along the Arkansas River border, running off livestock and killing whites. Demands for punishment of the Indians clashed with the pleas of Indian sympathizers in Washington, resulting in congressional establishment of the Indian Peace Commission of 1867. Meeting at Medicine Lodge (presently a town of the same name approximately one hundred miles southwest of Wichita), the Cheyennes and Arapahos agreed to allow safe passage of travelers and railroad construction through their lands. The treaty reduced their land to the area ceded by the Treaty of Little Arkansas that lay below the Kansas border, thus cutting Cheyenne territory to half its previous size. Twenty thousand dollars was to be spent annually for twenty-five years by the secretary of the Interior for what was thought to be beneficial to the tribes. Additional provisions of the treaty were the establishment of a permanent agency and compulsory schooling for the children. More food, blankets, and hardware were presented to the tribes than could be hauled away; among the government's presents was a considerable amount of ammunition.

Unfortunately, the Treaty of Medicine Lodge failed to bring a lasting peace. Battles continued between whites and warrior factions of the Cheyennes. In spite of the efforts of such peacemakers as Black Kettle, the zealous and aggressive Dog Soldier clan often engaged in violent episodes, which later brought tragedy to members of the peace faction of the Cheyennes. The behavior of the war faction of the Cheyennes might be explained by the "postulates" of Cheyenne cultural behavior identified by Hoebel. Among them are the following: "War is necessary to defend and advance the interests of the tribe. . . . War is necessary to permit individual self-expression and personality development of the male. . . . The individual personality is important" (99).

Within the individualistic Cheyenne system, it was impossible for only one chief such as Black Kettle to nullify opposing opinions within the tribe or enforce the entire tribe's cooperation with the terms of a given treaty. Neither was the U.S. government able to control the actions of its soldiers and citizens on the frontier. With the memory of Sand Creek only four years behind him, Black Kettle planned to relocate the 180 family lodges in his camp on the Washita River to a safer, more southerly site.

On November 27, 1868, the day of the camp's planned departure, cavalry under the command of Lt. Col. George Armstrong Custer attacked the camp to the accompaniment of Custer's signature tune, the Irish jig "Garry Owen," regimental musicians played it at Custer's request.[6] Black Kettle and his wife were found among the dead. The site of the battle, now

6. The traditional Irish jig tune "Garry Owen" is, to this day, associated with Custer to the extent that it is heard frequently as his theme in film scores. It is also the name of a town in Montana near the Custer Battlefield National Park.

named the Black Kettle National Grasslands, is located in central western Oklahoma near the Texas panhandle.

The Battle of the Washita was not the last tragic conflict between Cheyennes and whites, but a new peace policy established under the administration of President Ulysses Grant was an effort to ameliorate the situation. The policy came to be known as the "Quaker Peace Policy"; for positions as Indian agents, the secretary of the interior took nominations from religious groups with active evangelistic activities among the tribes. Grant specifically assigned two superintendencies to Quakers; these areas included Nebraska, Kansas, and the Indian Territory (Oklahoma).

Brinton Darlington established an agency (near present-day El Reno) within the new reservation; by an 1869 executive order, the reservation occupied land within the bounds of the Cherokee Outlet; the Cimarron River; the Kiowa, Comanche, and Kiowa-Apache reservation; and the state line of Texas. This jigsaw-shaped portion of land replaced the land assigned to the Cheyennes and Arapahos after the Treaty of Medicine Lodge two years before. The Cheyennes, resistant to Quaker evangelism, refused to send their children to the agency school or to take up farming. Still, Darlington was respected by the tribes, and until his death in 1872 the Cheyennes and whites enjoyed peaceful relationships and the buffalo robe trade prospered.[7]

Brinton Darlington was replaced by John D. Miles in 1872, and relations grew unstable in the next two years. Irritations grew as illegal whiskey, brought to the area through the exertions of incorrigible traders, caused disruption of home life and violent acts by those under its influence. By 1874 no buf-

---

7. The site of the Darlington Agency is now occupied by the Darlington State Game Bird Hatchery, north of El Reno.

falo could be found within a hundred miles of the agency. Hunger replaced prosperity and hostilities increased, setting the stage for a skirmish between a united force of five tribes against a white buffalo-hunting and -trading settlement.

At Adobe Walls (in present-day Hutchinson County, Texas) was a permanent encampment of hide hunters who had pushed into the territory assigned to the Comanches at Medicine Lodge. Faced with starvation if the buffalo were exterminated, the Indians in the area battled to resist the white hunters' further movement south. A combined war party of three hundred Cheyennes, Comanches, Kiowas, Apaches, and Arapahos fought in this battle, but were defeated. War parties of Southern Cheyennes continued to go to battle, but others surrendered at the Darlington Agency, where rations, mandatory schooling, government-issued Christianity, and instruction in farming awaited them.

The Northern Cheyennes, who had not accepted the reservation system begun with the Fort Laramie Treaty, continued to resist the white encroachment on the West; their battles of resistance would culminate in the famous battle of the Little Big Horn in 1876. In alliance with the Sioux, the Cheyennes decimated Custer's regiment; there were no white survivors. In spite of this victory, the Northern Cheyennes' military defeat was complete by 1878. John Seger, an employee of the Darlington Agency at the time, recorded these remarks:

> After the Custer battle, in which many Cheyennes were engaged, the authorities considered that if the warlike Northern Cheyennes were brought down to the agency and affiliated with their southern brethren, it would be easier to get them to take up the white man's ways. The northern division of the tribe agreed to do this, but as they afterwards said, it was with the understanding that if they did not like it in the south they could return north. At any rate, they were moved down to Darlington (27–28).

The Northern Cheyennes were unhappy at the southern reservation, and in September 1878, under the leadership of Little Wolf and Morning Star (also known as Dull Knife), they began an arduous trek back to their homeland, pursued by soldiers. The two groups subsequently took different directions, and Morning Star's group was arrested and confined at Fort Robinson (Nebraska) under inhumane conditions; their attempted escape in 1879 resulted in yet another massacre of Cheyennes. Little Wolf's group surrendered, was moved to Fort Keogh in Montana, and eventually settled near the Tongue River.[8]

After the return of the Northern Cheyennes to Montana, government agents in Oklahoma busied themselves with reeducating the Southern Cheyennes for existence within a society dominated by white cultural values. Government policymakers, committed to changing the economic structure of the Cheyennes from a system based on hunting to one based on agriculture, found that it was not possible to turn a Cheyenne into a replica of a white farmer in a matter of a few years. Finding themselves in the midst of an economic and social revolution, the Cheyennes faced life changes completely foreign to their culture.

Efforts were made to teach the Cheyennes and Arapahos about farming and animal husbandry, and some success was achieved in the latter; John Seger, then working at the agency school, was commended for his work with the schoolboys' growing herd. Miles reported that the Cheyennes were "industrious and energetic," ready to work as "laborers or as teamsters, or anything that will bring them a return in cash" (Berthrong, 91.)

8. The present-day Northern Cheyenne Reservation, which includes the cities of Busby and Lame Deer in Montana, occupies an area of approximately sixty square miles.

Although a newly founded teamster business allowed Indians from Darlington an opportunity to haul freight from Wichita to Darlington and various other agencies, their efforts were blocked by a threatened white competitor who diverted the freight. Looking for ways to make the Cheyenne and Arapaho reservation achieve self-sufficiency, Miles sought another avenue. Orchestrating an agreement between the Indians and members of the range cattle industry, grazing privileges were leased on acreages within the reservation. This attempt at yet another way of helping the tribes survive within the white economic system was a failure, and Miles resigned. The next agent, D. B. Dyer, returned to an emphasis on agriculture.

Dyer, reputed to be an inflexible man, ran into difficulties with a band of militant traditionalists who held out against the new way of life. Stock raising was failing because the Cheyennes were eating the cattle purchased with their grazing-permit payments. Dyer, who called the Cheyennes "ignorant, blanket Indians," believed they would never be able to be successful farmers. The reservation was in turmoil owing to disagreements between the cattlemen and Indians. In 1885 President Grover Cleveland ordered immediate removal of all cattlemen's herds from the reservation, and Dyer was removed as agent due to his lack of patience and tact.

Two schools had been built for the children on the reservation: Darlington was considered by the tribes to be the Arapaho school, and Caddo Springs, about a mile north, was attended by the Cheyennes. In 1879 the schools could accommodate only 25 percent of the agency children. Two other schools would open in the next few years: Cantonment School (near present-day Canton Lake) and a Mennonite mission school at Darlington. Some small groups of children were sent away to the Carlisle Indian School in Pennsylvania.

Beginning in 1879, David L. Payne and his followers "boomed" into the ears of Congress the idea of opening land in Indian Territory for settlement. Leading settlers into the Indian lands not yet officially assigned to specific tribes, Payne and his fellow homesteaders were evicted by troops and courts, but won support from sympathetic congressmen.[9] The Boomers' efforts led to the opening of the Unassigned Lands by Congress, and the Oklahoma Land Run of 1889 was the result. The lands of the Cheyennes and Arapahos were the next to be occupied; the stage was set by the Dawes Act of 1887.

The Dawes Act, also known as the General Allotment Act, gave the president of the United States the power to break down the reservations into small portions. The political bureaucracy decreed that each Indian on the Oklahoma Cheyenne and Arapaho reservation would be given "allotments in severalty," that is, discrete parcels of land to own as individuals. The surplus land would be opened to white settlement. Heads of families were to receive 160 acres, infants 40. The Southern Cheyennes resisted allotment, as did some Arapahos, who joined the Northern Arapahos at the Wind River Reservation in Montana rather than submit to allotment in severalty in Oklahoma.

To implement a policy that was not acceptable to the Cheyennes and Arapahos, various underhanded means were employed to acquire a sufficient number of tribe members' signatures required for legal ratification of the allotment of lands. Outside agitation by exacerbation of old feuds, falsification of documents, phony proxies, bribery, and threats were some of

9. "Boomers," a nickname for Oklahomans, derives from these early lobbyists' efforts to gain the attention of Congress. Another nickname, "Sooners," is also derived from the Land Run period, when some settlers tried to get ahead of other land competitors by not waiting for the gunshot (thereby "jumping the gun") that signaled the start of the run.

the tactics used by those who sought to defraud the Indians.[10] By these means, allotment in severalty was ratified, surplus lands were purchased by the government, and all annuities from the Medicine Lodge Treaty were canceled. April 19, 1892, was the date of the second run over Oklahoma Indian lands; in less than fifty years, the land inhabited and used by the Cheyenne and Arapaho tribes was reduced from millions to only 529,692 acres.

Between twenty-five thousand and thirty thousand settlers made the run. The Cheyennes and Arapahos were overwhelmed by contact with whites in bewildering numbers. In the six counties that had once been the reservation, they were in one day reduced to a distinct minority as 10 percent of the population. Considerable tension existed between the white settlers and the Indians; hostile actions occurred on both sides, but whites had a better chance in the courts of Indian Territory. Instances of Indians being fleeced by shrewd white businessmen were common in this era. Settlers unsatisfied with their land claims and jealous of what they perceived to be better lands held by Indians found an ally in territorial governor A. J. Seay, who advocated a liberal allotment-leasing policy that enabled white use of Indian allotments. According to the leasing agreements, non-Indians could use the land for three years but were required to fence it, dig wells, cultivate it, and make other improvements. This seemed to be an ideal situation for the Indians, because the whites could improve the land in ways the Indians had not yet learned, there was ready cash in the bargain, and after the three years they could repossess improved land. Unfortunately, the lessees came to feel that they had the

10. Moore reports that of the 464 signatures required for legal ratification, "only 146 can be verified from the official 1888 census" (210–13).

right to own the land because of their vested interest, and the legislature accommodated alienation of improved Indian allotments despite the Dawes Act, breaking the guarantee of a twenty-five-year trust period. Not only did unscrupulous maneuverings threaten the Indian's remaining land, but white cattlemen also ran their cattle unrestrained over Indian allotments.

During this time of social and political upheaval, many Cheyennes sought solace in a new religious movement that was awakening among the Plains tribes, crossing cultural boundaries, and uniting American Indians in a spiritual quest for a renewal of peace and prosperity remembered from the days before white invasion. Because Cheyenne spiritual life centered around the sun dance and arrow worship ceremonies, the Ghost Dance movement of the 1890s did not gain as strong a following among the Cheyennes as among other tribes. Nevertheless, the visions of the Paiute prophet Wovoka began a powerful movement that James Mooney described firsthand in an exhaustive document for the Bureau of Ethnography. "The great underlying principle of the Ghost Dance doctrine is that the time will come when the whole Indian race, living and dead, will be reunited upon a regenerated earth, to live a life of aboriginal happiness, forever free from death, disease and misery" (777). The first Ghost Dance ceremony held in the Indian Territory occurred on April 2, 1890.

Trances were a feature of the ceremonies, each vision producing a song. The songs of the Ghost Dance embodied the doctrine of the movement. In Oklahoma, as in other places across the nation, the faith in the movement began to die out after soldiers massacred 146 Sioux Ghost Dancers at Wounded Knee Creek in the Dakotas, prophecies of the return to past Indian glory went unfulfilled, and the peyote cult or newfound Christianity came to take the Ghost Dance's place in the religious life of the people.

At the time of allotment in severalty, only one out of five Cheyennes and Arapahos could speak the language of the people who were now the majority culture. Some Cheyennes lived in a traditional manner on their allotments, which frustrated the agents who tried to get them to accept white ways. A. E. Woodson, who became agent in 1893, tried to restrict all traditional activity. In 1899 the territorial legislature passed a bill forbidding the use of peyote; despite the legislation, the peyote cult endured. Tribal marriage customs also came under legal restriction, and the agency encouraged parents to send children to boarding school because Woodson wanted to keep them away from the camp as much as possible.

In 1896 Woodson forbade permission to the Cheyennes to hold the sun dance; in spite of the restriction, the Cheyennes held the ceremonies in 1898, with more than one thousand in attendance. Concerning their right to hold their traditional rites, the Cheyennes found allies in the ethnologists James Mooney and George A. Dorsey. The sun dance had for a long time been looked upon as evil by Christian missionaries; the Mennonite Rodolphe Petter considered it to be devil worship. In contrast, Dorsey and Mooney became involved in protecting the ceremonies from interference by the missionaries and the army.

The activities of Mooney and Dorsey at the turn of the century signal the beginning of a trend among American intelligentsia concerning the preservation of Indian traditions. The Arapaho Carl Sweezy remarked to his biographer, Althea Bass, concerning Mooney: "It was hard for us to realize, when he first came, that there were now people employed by the Government who believed that our art and history and religion had value, and that instead of stamping out everything Indian they must do what they could to understand and collect and record everything that belonged to our way of living" (62). This preservation mindset inspired the work of Natalie Curtis

(*The Indians' Book*) and later, in the 1930s, the work of Frances Densmore.

The attitude toward preservation exemplified by Mooney was not present, however, in the policies of government Indian agents in the early twentieth century. Woodson's goal was Indian self-sufficiency and assimilation into the white economic system through the destruction of traditional ways. But the Cheyennes were not inclined to give up their traditions and embrace a system in which success would be determined by the use of skills they had not yet developed. Unscrupulous merchants often took advantage of Indians' inexperience, and whiskey sellers took advantage of their frustration. In an effort to improve Indian agriculture, farmers were hired by the Cheyenne and Arapaho agency to give instruction in farming skills; the territory was divided into farm districts, each of which served as a subagency to meet local needs.

In 1906 Charles E. Shell became the disbursing agent and superintendent at Darlington. He combined the Darlington Arapaho School and the Caddo Spring Cheyenne schools into one; the school was called the Cheyenne and Arapaho School and was located at the Caddo Spring school site. Shell then changed the traditional name of Caddo Spring to Concho, naming it for himself in Spanish. School policy for many years forbade conversation among students in native languages or the singing of traditional songs; students who disobeyed these rules suffered restriction of activities or physical punishment.

The history of the Cheyenne nation in its relations with the United States government is a story of error and violence. The accommodating temperament of the Cheyenne people, which allowed them to live in harmony with the environment before the coming of Europeans to their land, aided them in their initial contacts with what was to become the dominant culture of America. The subsequent social and economic disturbance among the Cheyennes as a result of their contact with those who invaded their homeland was profound; the ramifications of the events of the first two centuries of contact are at the root of many contemporary tribal problems.

In spite of military attacks, shifting economic systems, and the often misguided efforts of agents and missionaries, the Cheyenne culture and people survived the nineteenth and twentieth centuries. Cheyenne culture and white American culture of the nineteenth and early twentieth centuries were incompatible; historical events illustrate that American diplomacy of that era was marked by intolerance of Indians based on ignorance of the possible validity of any other life model than the white American Christian pioneer farmer.

This overview of culture and history reveals the Cheyennes to be generous and spiritual people capable of valiant defense of their way of life through self-sacrifice and, when necessary, skilled fighting ability. Family life is closely knit, with children nurtured by multiple caretakers. Appreciation of the special gifts bestowed upon them from Ma hi yo, the creator god, finds expression in regularly observed traditional ceremonies as well as Christianized forms of worship.

At their tribal offices at Concho, Oklahoma, the Southern Cheyenne and Arapaho Tribes have a governing business committee of eight elected officials to direct expenditure of tribal funds and develop tribal programs. Ceremonial activity, however, is directed by the elders; the Sacred Arrows are renewed and the sun dance is celebrated annually. Whether Cheyenne spirituality is expressed in traditional religion, Native American Church ceremonies, Christianity, or everyday activity, the people are invigorated from within and enabled to face the challenges of living in two worlds: the world of traditional Cheyennes and the world of white culture.

A Cheyenne and Arapaho camp in the vicinity of Fort Reno (near modern-day El Reno and Concho, Oklahoma), circa 1890. The figure on the right is a woman wrapped in a blanket. (Photo 21, Shuck Collection, Western History Collections, University of Oklahoma Library)

Cheyenne family drying meat, July 4, 1895 (Photo 100, Campbell Collection, Western History Collections, University of Oklahoma Library)

Above left: Buffalo Meat, the composer of "I si Ni ha ni Jesus" (No. 24), great-grandfather of Rena Rose Youngbear. (Photo 42, Campbell Collection, Western History Collections, University of Oklahoma Library). **Top Right:** A Cheyenne woman, named Magpie, photographed with her children in front of her tipi around 1900. (Photo 175, Campbell Collection, Western History Collections, University of Oklahoma Library). **Bottom right:** These two unidentified Cheyenne girls in shawls (circa 1913) are standing in front of willow branches woven to make a shade for the camp. (Photo 155, Campbell Collection, Western History Collections, University of Oklahoma Library).

To the right of this tipi (circa 1900) there are poles used for hanging clothes. The poles might also have been used to make a baby swing. (Photo 57, Shuck Collection, Western History Collections, University of Oklahoma Library)

These girls on horseback were photographed in 1913. (Photo 2185, Campbell Collection, Western History Collections, University of Oklahoma Library)

Left: Frances Goose, grandmother of Joan Swallow and a composer of Cheyenne spiritual songs. See "Grandmother's Lullaby," No. 1, and "Grandmother's Story and Song," No. 28 (Photo 24, Sipe Collection, Western History Collections, University of Oklahoma Library). **Below left:** Woman Who Stands Aloof, circa 1935. She sang for Frances Densmore and was the companion of Bob-Tail Wolf at the time of the recording project. (Photo 127, Shuck Collection, Western History Collections, University of Oklahoma Library). **Below right:** Bob-Tail Wolf, Diane Hawk's great-great-grandfather and primary consultant for Densmore's 1936 project. (Photo 128, Shuck Collection, Western History Collections, University of Oklahoma Library).

Chapter Two

Lullabies and Children's Songs

When the creative act of Cheyenne song making happens, the song is not "composed"; people say it is "made." Sometimes singers know who made the song they sing, and sometimes no one knows—the songs have traveled the intricate routes of oral tradition from maker to singer. One of the songs in this chapter can be traced to a songmaker three generations removed from the present. Another song was made by the singer when she was a little girl. The rest belong to the realm of children's songs that have, through time, become the common property of Cheyenne childhood.

Cheyenne women are famous for their ability to put babies to sleep. Some Cheyenne consultants recalled witnessing lullaby-singing demonstrations at fairs in Oklahoma in decades past. In front of amazed country folk, crying babies were brought to a stand where a Cheyenne woman would sing and rock the baby to sleep. Observers testify that it worked.

About one lullaby, a singer commented, "That song don't belong to no tribe. It belongs to the baby." Three kinds of songs belonging to babies and children can be found in this chapter: songs used to put babies to sleep, game songs involving playful movements, and story songs.

Number 1
"Grandmother's Lullaby"
Joan Swallow, 2/5/91

1. *As spoken*

Baby da hii ssǫ
No gi yo zi̱
Nī o zi̱

2. *As sung*

A ma ho o o o o
Baby da hii **sso** hi yi
No gi yo **zi** yo zi yi
(Nau) o **zi** yo zi yi yi yi
A ma ho o o o
(Nau) o **zi** yo zi yi
Baby da hii **sso** hi yi
(Nau) o **zi** yo zi yi yi
A ma ho o o o
Baby da hii **sso** hi yi

3. *Translation*

Baby da hii ssǫ	—baby endearment; diminutive of "baby"
No gi yo zi̱	—alone; by yourself
Nī o zi̱	—sleep (command: "Go to sleep")

4. *Free translation*
_____

Little baby, you are alone to sleep.
Go to sleep.

Joan Swallow lives in Geary, Oklahoma. Her grandmother,
Frances Goose (now deceased), sang this song when Joan was
a child, and Joan believes that Frances made both the words
and the melody. Frances Goose, an active singer and maker of
Christian hymns, contributed five hymn texts and five texts
with music to the hymnal *Tsese-Maiheone-Nemeototse: Cheyenne Spiritual Songs* (Graber, 1982).

Joan explained that the syllables "a ma ho" were "like a
chant" with no definable meaning. But the words "Baby da hii
sso̱" recall warm memories of her grandmother calling Joan to
come to her. "Baby da hii sso̱" was a common pet name used
by mothers and grandmothers in past generations.

The word "no gi yo zi̱" (alone) has a more abstract meaning.
According to the translator Lenora Hart, the word communi-
cates the isolation of the baby in a peaceful place of sleep
within the surrounding, waking world.

Joan Swallow is a minister's wife who, like her grandmother,
makes spiritual songs and enjoys singing and encouraging
others to worship through music. Both Mrs. Goose's and Joan's
aural familiarity with the musical conventions of Western European hymnody might have influenced both the making and
the singing of "Grandmother's Lullaby" (no. 1).

This lullaby demonstrates two characteristics that are common to European folksong tradition: periodicity and tonal cen-
tricity resulting from a dominant–tonic relationship. The song
moves in phrases in a predictable pattern; it is the most peri-

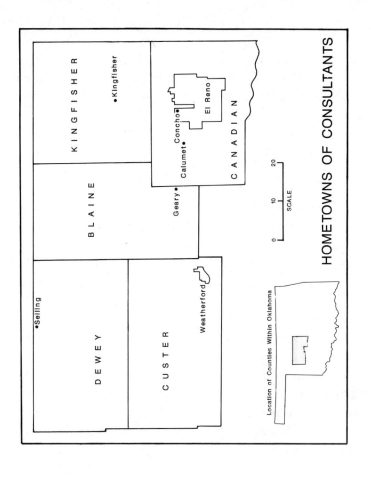

HOMETOWNS OF CONSULTANTS

odic of the four baby lullabies in this book. Only four tones are used: F, A flat, B flat, and C. Ascending from C and dipping down to C an octave lower, each phrase comes to rest on F. This emphasis on the dominant and tonic produces a feeling of tonal centeredness similar to the Western European dominant function. The other baby lullabies in this collection do not contain this particular dominant–tonic design.

A comparison between the text as it is spoken and as it is sung reveals an interesting recurring pattern. Many Southern Cheyenne words contain unvoiced or whispered vowel sounds. "Grandmother's Lullaby" contains three words with whispered vowels that are voiced in singing: "hii ss o̩," "no gi yo z i̩," and "nī o z i̩" (see Fig. 1). The act of singing forms new syllables on the ends of words that have unvoiced endings in spoken Cheyenne.

The word endings, ordinarily unvoiced, that are transformed to new syllables when sung are highlighted in the written text by italicized boldface type (see **sso** and **zi** on page 45). Vocables that are not part of definable words are merely italicized (see *a, ma, ho,* etc.).

The syllable within parentheses (nau) has been altered by a vowel change when sung. In this song, this adjusted vowel sound replaces the first syllable of "nī o z i̩" with "nau." The difference between the two sounds is distinctive and interesting, and a possible reason for the change might have to do with vocal technique.

It is possible to make vowel changes in words when singing to produce a more resonant sound, using the voice more efficiently for volume. In this case, the change of "nī" to "nau" accommodates a lift of the soft palate, resulting in a more open vocal sound and less physiological strain on the vocal mechanism. Joan Swallow has enjoyed singing since child-hood and is from a musical family; she sings before large groups at revivals, funerals, and church services. The personal techniques she has developed to increase her vocal volume without added strain might include the practice of modified vowels to accommodate the sound she desires. Whether or not this is the case, the change of "nī" to "nau" is aurally distinctive and is a personal vocal signature.

Figure 1. Cheyenne Orthography

This chart is based on the pronunciation key from "Modern Southern Cheyenne" by Lenora Hart, Department of Education, Southern Cheyenne and Arapaho Tribes, Concho, Oklahoma. Correspondence with English vowels is approximate.

Vowels[1]

a	as in t*a*lk or c*a*ll
a̱	*a* blended with preceding consonant and whispered
i	as in p*i*t
ī	as in the pronoun *I*
i̱	*i* blended with preceding consonant and whispered
o	as in h*o*ly
ô	as in *ou*ght; also written as *au* as in n*au* gi (we do)
o̱	*o* blended with preceding consonant and whispered
u	as in m*u*ltiply
ə	English schwa sound as in b*a*nan*a* (bənanə)
ə̱	schwa blended with preceding consonant and whispered appearing over two vowels indicates upward change in pitch

Consonants

b	used interchangeably with *p*
d	as in *d*ome; used interchangeably with *t*

1. "The short vowel sounds [*i, o, u*] are shorter than the English sounds. The long vowel sounds are about the same as the English sounds; however, where there is a double vowel [*ii, oo*] the sound is slightly longer" (Hart, 3).

g	as in gig (sounded softly)
h	as in *h*ot
k	as in *k*eep
kha	as in a blend of *c*all and *h*a (soft palate)
khi	as in blend of *k* with *c*all and *h*i (high soft palate)
kho	as in blend of *k* with *c*all and *h*o (soft palate)[2]
m	as in *m*ine
mha	*m*a blended with *h*a (through nose)
mhi	*m*a blended with *h*i
n	as in *n*o
p	soft *p* as in *p*ivot
s	sharp sound as in *s*o
ss	soft sound as in ni*c*e
ssh	soft sound as in *sh*e
sh	sharper sound, almost as in *ch*ip but with stress on *s*
sk	as in a*sk*
t	as in *t*alk; used interchangeably with *d*
v	as in *v*ivid
vh	blend of *v* and *h* to sound like *wh*oa but with distinct *v* sound[3]
y	as in *y*odel or bo*y*
z	as in pi*ts*, or doubled as a separate syllable (yo zz zi)

2. The distinctions between *kha, khi,* and *kho* are difficult for the non-Cheyenne ear to perceive. The sounds are much like the *ch* in the German *Bach*. Lenora Hart has noted that Germans can learn to speak Cheyenne well.
3. Some Cheyennes pronounce *v* as *w*. Several shades of difference between the two consonants can be heard in different people's speech.

Number 2
"Lullaby for Gray Eyes"
Wilma Blackowl Hamilton, 10/2/90

1. *As spoken*

> Baby das, Baby dass on,
> Gii dai̲ ma mi das, Baby das,
> Gii dai̲ ma mi das, Gii dai̲ ma mi das,
> ma zi̲ mioz das.

2. *As sung*

> *Ma ho ho* Baby das son *o ho,*
> *Ma ho, ma ho, ho ma ho,*
> Baby das *so* son *o ho,*
> Gii da ma mi das son *o ho,*
> *Ma ho, ma ho, ho ma ho,*
> Baby das *so* son *o ho,*
> Gii da ma mi das son *o ho,*
> Ma ho, ma ho, ho ma ho, ma ho,
> Gii da ma mi das son *o ho,*
> *Ma ho, ma ho, ho ma ho, ma ho.*
> Gii da ma mi das son *o ho,*

Ma zi mi o das *so,* son *o ho,*
Ma ho, ma ho, ho ma ho, ma ho.

3. *Translation*

Baby das	— derived from "baby da so," an endearing name for baby (as "Baby das *so* son *o ho,*" perhaps derived from "baby dass on", plural form of baby endearment)
gii da i̲	— endearing name for little boy
ma mi das	— added to "gii da i̲," intensifies endearment; word; possibly refers to eye ("ma i khi")* and big (prefix "ma"),† therefore explaining singer's translation of "gii da ma mi das" as "little boy with big eyes"
ma zi̲	— turd
mi oz	— smells
da so	— endearment

4. *Free translation*

My little baby, my little boy, my little stinker.
(Wilma's translation: "Little boy with big
eyes, with a full diaper.")

---

*Cheyenne-English Bilingual Institute, *Ni zhi si ni ss zi,* 6.
†Northern Cheyenne Language and Culture Center, *English-Cheyenne Student Dictionary,* 8. The entries "big store," "Bighorn Mountains," and "Bighorn River" all begin with "ma'."

"Lullaby for Gray Eyes" (no. 2) was sung by Wilma Blackowl Hamilton of Calumet, Oklahoma. Wilma is a homemaker, mother, and grandmother and serves as a matron at the Riverside Indian School in Anadarko, Oklahoma. In the past, Wilma, like her mother, Margaret, participated in dance competitions as a fancy dancer, which makes both of them pioneers among the slowly growing number of women who have adopted this traditionally male dance style. Wilma learned this song from her grandmother, Susie Blackowl of El Reno, now deceased.

As in the previous lullaby, the vocables "ma" and "ho" are used frequently. The melody is repetitive and is marked by a recurring rhythmic motive that has been transcribed as an eighth note slurred to a dotted quarter tied to another quarter (see mm. 3–4). This motive begins with a slight accent and decreases in volume quickly; the dynamic changes within each occurrence of the motive produce a quiet but strong rhythmic feeling.

Phrases are punctuated by relaxed breaths; the majority of the phrases end on G, as does the last phrase. Only two other pitches appear: A and C. Because of the position of G at the end and at the end of phrases, the other notes seem to act as pivotal notes, always turning the melody back to G. For these reasons, G seems to be the tonal center of the lullaby.

Wilma explained that this lullaby is supposed to be sung to boy babies ("gii da i̱" is an endearment for little boys), but she had also sung this song to her daughters. When asked about the meaning of the song, Wilma said, "It's just about a little baby that has big eyes, with a full diaper." The joking but tender endearment "ma zi̱ mi oz das" (a diminutive form of "turd smells") may be freely translated as "little stinker."

While singing, Wilma rocked her baby grandson, "Gray Eyes." On the tape sounds from the baby can be heard from time to time along with the swish of clothes and pats to the diaper. The lullaby was effective; during Wilma's song, he fell asleep.

Number 3
"Lullaby"
Imogene Jones, 2/5/91

Ma – ho –, Ma ho – ho,

Ma – ho – ho ho,

1. *As Spoken*

Vocables: *ma, ho*

2. *As Sung*

Vocables: *ma, ho*

3. *Translation*

The vocables *ma* and *ho* appear in all of the lullabies (with the exception of "Kitten Lullaby") I collected. These syllables are considered by Imogene Jones to have the function of soothing the baby, who "knows you are there to rock it."

4. *Free Translation*

Soothing vocable sounds

Imogene Jones works to help recovering alcoholics and drug addicts at the tribe's halfway house. A member of the Cheyenne and Arapaho Language Group, she sang this "Lullaby" (no. 3) at an evening meeting in February 1991. Imogene stated, "This is what they used to hum a long time ago for small babies when they would rock them back and forth. . . . It's just a little tune that goes over and over and it's supposed to put the baby to sleep and soothe the baby, knowing that you are there to rock it."

The song is a simple chant with a range of three pitches (F, G, and A flat). Each phrase of the chant returns to F, the lowest of the pitches. The text of the lullaby consists of only two vocables: "ma" and "ho." The three phrases display an interesting cumulative effect: the first phrase iterates the vocable "ho" once, the second phrase twice, and the third phrase, three times.

This song is also distinguished by its half steps in the melody line, chromatic flavor that gives it a distinct melodic difference from the Wilma's and Joan's. The next lullaby is particularly chromatic, with a line of three half steps extending for two and a half beats (at half note = 70).

Number 4
"Lullaby for a Nursing Baby"
Bertha Little Coyote, 3/14/91

Number 4
"Lullaby for a Nursing Baby"
Bertha Little Coyote, 3/14/91

1. *As spoken*

   Vocables: *a, ma, ho*

2. *As sung*

   Vocables: *a, ma, ho*

3. *Translation*

   These syllables appear in all of the
   lullabies in this collection (with the exception of "Kitten Lullaby").

4. *Free translation*

   Bertha Little Coyote calls this text "just
   chant."

   Bertha Little Coyote has fond memories of "Lullaby for a
Nursing Baby" (no. 4)—she sang to her baby son in 1931. At
that time, Bertha says, bottle feeding was uncommon. Bertha
breast-fed her baby, rocking him from side to side in a pivoting
motion (rather than back and forth as in a rocking chair) while
she sang: "We'd sing [the lullaby]. . . . Just keep repeating like
that, and I guess it was music to them, no words in it. It was
just the melody, they liked that, and they'd go to sleep."
   This peaceful lullaby has a notable rhythmic pulse. Regular
vocal stresses recur on the first note of eighth-plus-dotted-

Figure 2. Notation Symbols Used in Transcriptions

 F sharp throughout; no key or scale implication

 pitch lowered by no more than a quarter tone

 portamento into note from above

 portamento into note from below

 portamento fades downward to indeterminate pitch

 portamento between notes

 indeterminately pitched slide downward

 indeterminately pitched slide upward

recognizable quickly released pitch occurring before a note; a grace note

 indeterminate vocal pitch; also used to notate instruments of indeterminate pitch

 slur indicating sustained syllable

 tie and dash under second note indicating sustained syllable

 indicates the repulsation of a tone without repeating the tone

 accent

 note quickly released

 segno; a mark of location for reference in commentary

quarter units. The first two phrases are repeated, with the last note lengthened on the repeat. [At measure 5 an intriguing chromatic passage begins with an upward leap from A to F, followed by a descent (including two adjacent half-step intervals) back to A at the end of the phrase.] The remaining phrases are similar to the first two, but in reversed order.

This lullaby is interesting in both melodic and formal aspects. I have transcribed "Lullaby for a Nursing Baby" and several other low-lying songs in the bass clef, rather than the treble clef normally used for women's voices, when excessive leger lines would have competed with the text underlay for space (see Fig. 2 for other aspects of the notation). In the case of this song, the bass clef transcription allows the chromatic descending phrase in measure 5 to be seen easily. The phrase sounds uncaracteristic in comparison to the other songs in this book, most melodies examined do not contain such conjunct melodic material. The last phrase's resemblance to the first phrase provides a sense of return to the form of the lullaby.

Because of the recurrence of "ma" and "ho" (especially the combination "ma ho") in all of the Cheyenne lullabies I had heard, and because of the hushed and reverent singing style, I asked Bertha if there might be a connection between the chant syllables "ma ho" and the Cheyenne word "Ma hi yo" (God). The possibility was interesting to her and seemed plausible. If so, this is an example of an evolution of vocables from a definable word. Taking into consideration the reverence of the Cheyenne cultural personality, it is possible that prayers of thanksgiving and protection for an infant might be at the root of the lullaby's vocables.

Number 5
"Kitten Lullaby"
Mary Lou Stone Road Prairie Chief, 2/5/91

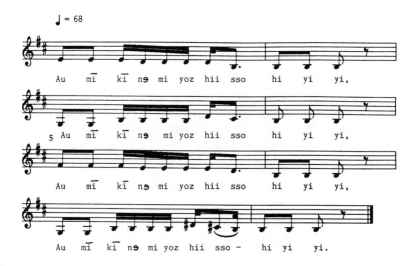

1. *As spoken*

   Kī nii yo zi̱ hii ssǫ

2. *As sung*

   Au mī kī nə *mi* yoz hii **sso** *hi yi yi*
   Au mī kī nə *mi* yoz hii **sso** *hi yi yi*
   Au mī kī nə *mi* yoz hii **sso** *hi yi yi*
   Au mī kī nə *mi* yoz hii **sso** *hi yi yi*

3. *Translation*

kī nii yo zi̱ — tired
hii ssọ   — diminutive

4. *Free Translation*

My little tired one,
My little tired one,
My little tired one,
My little tired one.

Mary Lou Stone Road Prairie Chief, a fond grandmother as well as a social worker, takes great pride in her full-blood Cheyenne heritage. She has also served as chairperson of the Cheyenne and Arapaho Language Group, organized to preserve language and customs through regular conversation, vocabulary collection, and story swapping.

Mary Lou made this song when she was a little girl playing with her cats:

When I lived out in the country, I was raised by my grandma and grandpa, and didn't have . . . storebought dolls. Mine were what we made—rag dolls. I had a lot of cats, and I would take them and I would bathe them every day. And they tell me that cats don't like water. But I would bathe them every day and then I would *ho hũ do,* I would wrap them like you do a baby and I would lay them in the sun. And there were, I think I had five little kittens and then the mother cat. The mother cat wouldn't let me do that to her, but the little kittens would. And I would get the little kittens and put them on my shoulder.

The "Kitten Lullaby" (no. 5) is the song Mary Lou would sing while holding her wrapped-up kittens.

According to Mary Lou, the only translatable word in the text is the word for "tired," sung by her as "kī nə mi yoz," with the diminutive "hii ssǫ" added. Mary Lou's "kī nǝ mi yoz" is a variation of the Cheyenne word "kī nii yo zi̱" (tired). The rest of the sounds are considered by Mary Lou to be vocables.

The first two vocables, "au mī," sound a great deal like the English words "oh my," which when pronounced with an Oklahoma accent sound like "aw ma." Since Mary Lou was a small child when she made up this song, it seems possible that her childish accents in both Cheyenne and English transformed "Oh my kī nii yo zi̱" (Oh, my tired one) into "Au mī kī nǝ mi yoz hii ꞏ ssǫ" (Oh, my little tired one). Whether or not this is the case, Mary Lou's vocal style differed from the other songs she sang for this project; for the "Kitten Lullaby" Mary Lou used an ingenuous childlike tone quality, pitched in a small child's vocal range.

The words "kī nǝ mi yoz hii ssǫ" follow a similar rhythmic pattern when sung as when spoken, with an accent on the "hii" of "hii sso" reflected in the sixteenth-note-plus-dotted-eighth transcription. Each phrase is five beats long, which would be considered a recurring irregularity in a Western European folksong.

Another interesting musical aspect within "Kitten Lullaby" is its melodic content. Each of its four phrases ends with the vocables "hi yi yi" on the pitch B; the first three phrases contain the pitches G, B, C sharp, D, E, and F sharp. The last phrase introduces an aural surprise in the form of D sharp (m. 7) in the place of D natural in the corresponding measures (mm. 1, 3, and 5). This melodic device gives the melody an interest that the expected D natural would not provide, and is perhaps a subtle musical joke invented by a clever little girl.

Number 6
"Rabbit Song"
Rhoda Young Bird Braxton, 1/19/91

1. *As spoken* (by translator Lenora Hart)

Vo go hii sso̱
Hos ssta ha mi̱
Na ho da o vi̱
Baby
Vo go, vo go, vo go

2. *As sung* (by Rhoda)

Vo go hii **sso**
Hos ssta *ma hi*
A no da va hi
Baby *no zi i va hi*
Vo go, vo go, vo go!

3. *Translation*

vo go	— rabbit
hii sso̱	— little; diminutive (vo go hii so̱—little rabbit)
hos ssta ha mi̱	— threw me out
na	— I/me
ho da o vi̱	— threw out
zi i vi	— leave

4. *Free translation*

Little rabbit, little rabbit,
Threw me out, kicked me!
Little rabbit, little rabbit, little rabbit!

"Rabbit Song" (no. 6), recorded in the home of Rhoda Young Bird Braxton of Kingfisher, Oklahoma, in January 1991, is both a baby-bouncing song and a children's game. Rhoda learned it when her mother sang the song to Rhoda's children: "She sang it to us and she made a game out of it, you know. And we had to put four fingers on each side of the head [two on each side] and make like a rabbit and then dance around . . . and we used to make the babies jump up and down." Rhoda pantomimed bouncing a baby up and down on her lap as she sang, with a large bounce on the final "vo go!" When children are bigger, this song turns into a musical game for hopping around on the floor.

Rhoda was unable to translate the text of "Rabbit Song" except for "vo go" (rabbit); she had learned the song by rote. Lenora Hart, who had heard the song in her childhood, translated "Rabbit Song." A comparison between the rote-learned words and the words remembered by Lenora indicates that the text that appears here is a product of alteration by oral transmission. For example, "hos ssta ha mi̱" (threw me out) becomes "hos ssta *ma hi*"; "na ho da o vi̱" (kicked me) becomes "*a no da va hi*." The line "Baby *no zi i va hi*," according to Hart, may be related to the word "zi i vi" (leave), as in "he left"; this line is obscure.

"Rabbit Song" contains an interesting rhythmic contrast between phrases; the rhythm of the melody seems to match the sense of the text. The first phrase falls into a regular triple meter, introducing the "vo go hi sso̱" (little rabbit). The song changes in both meter and beat length at measure 6; duple meter accompanies the text words "kicked me" and "left me." The bouncy, triple rhythmic quality returns with the fourth phase (m. 12) on the word "vo go" (rabbit).

The scale of "Rabbit Song" is pentatonic, with E flat as the tonal center. The melody begins on E flat, departs for a new center, B flat, returns to E flat, and finally ascends to an indeterminate tone on the last syllable of "vo go."

The text is ambiguous: which person, the rabbit or the baby, does the throwing out, kicking, and leaving? The matter is further obscured by the motion of the baby bouncing into the air on the last "vo go"; perhaps this is the rabbit throwing the baby out.

Another consideration is the old Cheyenne practice of dressing babies in rabbit fur diapers; a furry-bottomed baby might be acting the part of a rabbit being thrown up in the air. Rabbit fur diapers were not washed but thrown away when soiled. Here might be yet another clue to the meaning of "threw me out," and is possibly the second scatological but affectionate reference found among these Cheyenne baby songs.

Number 7
"Little Warty Lullaby"
Mary Armstrong, 9/18/90

1. *As spoken*

Shi sh gi ma, shi sh gi ma,
Nī o zi̱.
Shi sh gi ma, shi sh gi ma,
Nī o zi̱.

2. *As sung*

Shi shgi ma, shi shgi ma,
(Nau) o *zi* so ho.
Shi shgi ma, shi shgi ma,
(Nau) o *zi* so ho.

3. *Translation*

shi sh gi ma —wart
nī o zi̱   — sleep (command: go to
            sleep)

4. *Free translation*

Wart, wart, go to sleep.
Wart, wart, go to sleep.
According to Mary Armstrong:
"Little wart, little warty, go to sleepy, go
to sleepy.
Little wart, little warty, go to sleepy, go to
sleepy."

"Little Warty Lullaby" (no. 7) was sung by Mary Armstrong
in her home in Geary, Oklahoma. Mary is highly respected for
her spiritual role in the Oklahoma Cheyenne community, and
was a consultant to David Graber and his colleagues in the
compilation of *Tsese-Ma'heone-Nemeotótse: Cheyenne Spiritual Songs.*

Mary was educated at Concho Indian Boarding School (now
closed). At the school, Mary was not allowed to speak Cheyenne, and once had her mouth washed out with yellow soap
when she broke the rule. Paradoxically, one of the songs Mary
remembers being taught in her boarding school music class
was called "Navajo Lullaby"; yet she was restricted from singing Cheyenne songs.

Mary lives a simple life and participates in the tribe's traditional religious ceremonies as a ceremonial instructor. Concerning Cheyenne traditions, she is possibly one of the most
knowledgeable women alive today. A skilled beadworker, Mary
produces moccasins, beaded buckskin dresses, and other arti-
cles that are in high demand both within the Cheyenne community and among collectors.

When we visited together, Mary described the old-fashioned

practice of using rope cradles for babies. Doorposts, trees, or posts around the camping grounds (such as those used to erect traditional shaded kitchens at the sun dance) held ropes that suspended a soft padding of blankets. Babies were placed in these rope swing cradles, given an occasional push, and lulled to sleep in a breezy safe place out of the line of adult traffic (see the photograph on page 41).

"Little Warty Lullaby" is the type of song Mary has used to put little babies to sleep. Others have described this lullaby as a bedtime game. Diane Hawk of Kingfisher remembers playing a pinching game with her grandmother and singing this song. Diane and her grandmother (and any other children present) would stack up their hands, palms down, in single pile, alternating hands. Each person would then take a pinch of the skin of the hands underneath their own hands. Diane relates: "Grandma would pinch our hands real easy, so as not to hurt us. But because of the loose skin on Grandma's hands, we could get a real good pinch—almost a handful!" Several other consultants have fond memories of singing this bedtime play song, gently shaking the pile of pinched hands in rhythm with the song. After the song would end, the hand pile broke up and the players would tickle each other in the midriff area.

The text of "Little Warty Lullaby" contains both altered vowels and voiced vowels that would be whispered in ordinary speech. The Cheyenne word "nī o zi̠" (go to sleep) is altered to "nau o zi" when Mary sings it. As in "Grandmother's Lullaby," the syllable "nī" is vocally adjusted to "nau"; "zi̠" is altered to "zi."

The melody consists of two identical phrases separated by a breath of nonspecific length (represented by slash marks after m. 8). Other than the pause for breath, the entire melody has a regular triple rhythm. The pitch index consists of F sharp, A, and B; F sharp appears to be the tonal center. The descending minor third in the middle and at the end of each phrase (A to F sharp) is a teasing motive found in many children's songs throughout the world.

The minor third interval plays an important role in all of the lullabies, the two "wart" songs, and the "Mud Hen" songs at the end of this chapter. Bruno Nettl has stated that the minor third is one of the most common intervals found in Plains music, and that dotted rhythms are also very common.

Number 8
"Tickling Song"
Imogene Jones, Mary Lou Stone Road Prairie
Chief, Joan Swallow, 2/5/91

Shi shgi ma,   shi shgi ma,   hi   yi   yi,   shi shgi ma,

shi shgi ma   hi   yi   yi.

1. *As spoken*

   Shi sh gi ma, shi sh gi ma,
   Shi sh gi ma, shi sh gi ma,

2. *As sung*

   Shi shgi ma, shi shgi ma,
   Hi yi yi,
   Shi shgi ma, shi shgi ma,
   Hi yi yi.

3. *Translation*

   shi sh gi ma—wart

4. *Free translation*

   Wart, wart,
   Wart, wart.

"Tickling Song" (no. 8), sung for me by the trio of Imogene Jones, Mary Lou Stone Road Prairie Chief, and Joan Swallow, is a playground game like the pinching game of "Little Warty Lullaby." In this game, children pile up their hands in alternation and pinch the skin of the hand below. While singing, the children would gently shake the hands as a group, being careful not to break the communal pinch. At the end of the song, all hands break away and tickling hilarity begins.

The text of the song has only one word, "shi shgi ma" (wart), and two vocables ("hi" and "yi"). The chant is based solely on the common childhood teasing interval of a minor third. The repeated A naturals at the ends of the phrases on the vocables "hi yi yi" establish a tonal center. Dotted-eighth-and-sixteenth patterns add to the joking quality. "Little Warty Lullaby" and "Tickling Song" tell us that warts are fun to sing about and are acceptable as pet names for Cheyenne babies.

Number 9
"Mud Hen Song No. 1"
Joan Swallow, 2/5/91

Number 9
"Mud Hen Song No. 1"
Joan Swallow, 2/5/91

1. *As spoken*

Zi mo ma ǫ go in
Zi do dōō yo zz zi

2. *As Sung*

Four times:
Zi mo ma' go i'
Zi do do' do yo zi *hi yi*

3. *Translation*

zi	— they
mo ma ǫ go in	— condition of eye infection (ma ǫ—red)
do dōō	— open
yo zz zi	— eyes

4. *Free translation*

They will have red eyes who open their eyes.

Number 10
"Mud Hen Song No. 2"
Imogene Jones and Joan Swallow, 2/5/91

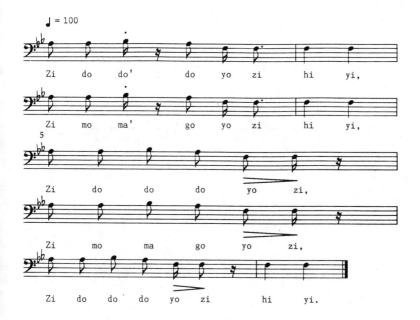

1. *As spoken*

    Zi do do͞o yo zz zi,
    Zi mo ma ǫ go in yo zz zi.

2. *As Sung*

    Zi do do' *do* yo zi, *hi yi,*
    Zi mo ma' go yo zi, *hi yi,*
    Zi do do' *do* yo zi,

Zi mo ma' go yo zi,
Zi do do' *do* yo zi, *hi yi.*

3. *Translation*

zi	— they
do dō͞o	— open
yo zz zi	— eyes
ma o̧	— red
mo ma o̧ go in	— condition of eye infection (ma o—red)

4. *Free translation*

They who open their eyes will have red eyes.

Number 11
"Mud Hen Song No. 3"
Imogene Jones, 2/5/91

Number 11
"Mud Hen Song No. 3"
Imogene Jones, 2/5/91

1. *As Spoken:*

Zi do do͞o yo zz zi,
Zi mo ma ǫ go in yo zz zi.

2. *Song Words as Sung:*

Zi do do' *do* yo zi, *hi yi,*
Zi mo ma' go yo zi, *hi yi,*
Zi do do' *do* yo zi,
Zi mo ma' go yo zi, *hi yi,*
Zi do do' *do* yo zi, *hi yi,*
Zi do do' do yo zi̲, Zi do do *do* yo zi,
Zi mo ma' go yo zi, *hi yi.*

3. *Word for Word Translation:*

zi	— they
do do͞o	— open
yo zz zi	— eyes
ma ǫ	— red
mo ma ǫ go in	— condition of eye infection (ma o—red)

4. *Free Translation of Song Text:*

They who open their eyes will have red eyes.

The "Mud Hen Songs Nos. 1–3" are three song variants forming part of a story told by Mary Lou Stone Road Prairie Chief and recorded at the February meeting of the Cheyenne and Arapaho Language Group. Two other versions of this story, "Why the Mudhen Has Red Eyes," have been published in *Náévahóo'ohtséme/We Are Going Back Home: Cheyenne History and Stories*.[1] The following is a transcription from the field tape of Mary Lou's story, which she told in English:

> This story I'm about to recite is about prairie dogs and a mud hen, or prairie dogs and mud hens. There was a *vi ho i,* a white man, and he was walking down the road. And as he was going down the road he seen this mud hen, and these prairie dogs were walking on side of him, and they asked him—he had a bundle on his back—and so they asked him what was in the bundle. And he wouldn't tell them, he would just explain to them that he was on his way somewhere, that he was going somewhere. And they kept asking him, "What's in the bundle on your back?" And he said, "Well, my songs are in there. I have some songs in there." So they told him, "Well, let me look, let us see your songs, let us hear your songs!" And he said, "No, I can't do it, they're sacred songs, I can't let anybody hear them, they're sacred songs." So as he went on, they kept asking him. So finally he told them, "OK, OK, you talked me into it, I'll sing my songs. But before I sing my songs, I want you to know that they are sacred songs, and that I don't just sing them for anybody, and that I want you to get in a circle, but you gotta dance for me as I sing. So they all agreed and he said, "Form a circle, and as I sing, I want you to kind of sway back and forth. But I want to remind you that they are sacred songs and I don't want you—you can't

1. Wayne Leman, ed., *Návévahóo'ohtséme/We Are Going Back Home: Cheyenne History and Stories Told by James Shoulderblade and Others,* 362–68. According to Leman, this story also appears in other Algonquian languages. The stories in *Náévahóo'ohtséme* are printed in Cheyenne with interlinear English translation.

open your eyes. I want you to close your eyes, and when I start singing everybody has to keep your eyes closed."

So as he began to sing, they began to sway back and forth and they were dancing, and the mud hen, as he began to sway back and forth, well, he kind of felt an empty space next to him. He could feel one side, but he couldn't feel the other side. And as he continued dancing, well, after a while, then he couldn't feel anything on the other side either. So he took a couple of steps over and swayed again and he still couldn't feel nobody. And about this time he began to get alarmed and he began to wonder what was going on, so he opened his eyes, and when he opened his eyes, he saw the white man was killing them. Which in effect, the man had been hungry, and he seen this as a way to get him something to eat without him having to go hunting or anything. But the song says "If you open your eyes, your eyes will turn red." That's why today mudhens have red eyes. This is a Cheyenne—I don't know whether you would call it a fairy tale, but it's just a Cheyenne tale. And this is the song that goes with what I just recited.

After Mary Lou told the story at the language group meeting, three different "Mud Hen" songs could be recalled by group members. Song No. 1 can be freely translated as "They will have red eyes who open their eyes." The others have the same free translation: "They who open their eyes will have red eyes." Lenora Hart defines "mo ma o go in" as a condition of redness of the whites of the eyes, as when one has not slept or is intoxicated.

The red-eyed mud hen is a medium-size freshwater fowl often found in the company of ducks, although not a member of the duck family. The bird is common to Oklahoma and has a specified hunting season. The mud hen is also referred to as "coot" and "doule d'eau"; it is not, in modern times, prized for game because of what has been described as a muddy, fishy taste. Both males and females have red eyes, and some say that the mud hens' eyes become redder in mating season.

"Mud Hen Song No. 1," sung by Joan Swallow alone, is the one she remembers from her childhood. It contains an interesting rhythmic motive based on the rhythm of the text words "zi do dōͨ" (they open), which becomes "do do'" when sung. The dotted eighth and sixteenth-note motive that accompanies "zi do do'" adds to the rhythmic drive of the song. Shortening occurs in another place with the word "mo ma o̧ go in" (redness of the eyes) to the sung "mo ma go i'," resulting in a glottal stop after "ma'" and "i'." Shortened words with glottal stops are heard in all of the "Mud Hen" songs.

Song No. 1 moves in a pattern of alternating three-beat and five-beat units. The melody contains four pitches (E, G, A, and C), with each phrase ending with vocables ("hi yi") on E. The other "Mud Hen" songs follow the same pattern of all phrases ending on the lowest pitch.

"Mud Hen Song No. 2," sung by Joan Swallow and Imogene Jones, was remembered by both as an alternate version to the one they each knew best. It contains a jumpy rhythmic "snap" on the word for eyes: "yo zz i" (sung "yo zi"). The final syllable of "yo zi" is very quiet in both songs, almost seeming to disappear at times. An alteration of three-beat versus two-beat units occurs through measures 1–4; measures 5 and 6 are both three-beat units, followed by a return to the three/two pattern of the beginning. Three pitches are contained in the melody: A flat, B flat, and F. The relation between the first and last notes of each phrase is a minor third, a pattern shared with the other two songs.

"Mud Hen Song No. 3," sung by Imogene Jones with backup from Joan Swallow, was the one Imogene's grandmother used to sing. In both nos. 2 and 3, the word "mo ma o̧ go in" has been shortened to "mo ma' go." Song no. 3 corresponds to no. 2 for the first six measures, after which the vocables "hi yi" signal new material. The remainder of the song is composed of a different arrangement of the same melodic units found in the previous song.

George Herzog, in a study of animal story songs among several American Indian tribes, found animal story songs to be often brief; simple in melody, rhythm, and structure; composed of one or two phrases; a fifth or less in range; constituted of two to four tones; unaccompanied; often "chanted forms of spoken sentences, on the borderline of music"; devoid of strings of vocables, with the music supporting definable words within the song; often found in trickster stories.[2] The "Mud Hen" songs conform to all of these characteristics except range (a sixth rather than a fifth.)

OTHERS LOOK AT CHEYENNE BABY SONGS

Around the turn of the century, Natalie Curtis, author of *The Indians' Book,* transcribed a lullaby, the first notated Oklahoma Cheyenne baby song: "Meshivotzis-o, naotziyo tsiso" (Little good baby, sleepy little baby) sung for her by Wihunahe (Chief Woman) (160). The first phrase of Chief Woman's lullaby sounds similar to "Grandmother's Lullaby," and it has other striking similarities to the lullabies in this chapter: dotted rhythmic motives, limited range (three pitches), and nonuniform phrase lengths. In Chief Woman's text, the similarity between the word Curtis wrote as "naotziyo" and Joan Swallow's "nī o zi̱" (sleep) is evident, as is the resemblance between "tsiso" and "hi sso̱" (little).

In the light of what Natalie Curtis learned from Chief Woman at the turn of the century, and what I have learned from Cheyenne women in the 1990s, it is surprising to read a curious observation from Frances Densmore (1936). "There are no

2. George Herzog, "Special Song Types in North American Indian Music," *Zeitschrift für vergleichende Musickwissenschaft* (Berlin), 3 (1935): 9.

lullabies among the Cheyenne, as the crooning to little children is not dignified by the name of singing. A man, however, sings war songs or the songs of men's dances to his little son or grandson." In contrast, my friend Bertha Little Coyote said this about "Lullaby for a Nursing Baby": "This is an Indian lullaby that we used to sing to our babies back in 1931, when I had my son, and they used to sing these little Indian lullabies. . . . There's other baby songs, too, but this one has no words in it."

Many Cheyennes in Oklahoma feel regret that many women who knew "the old songs" are deceased. We are particularly fortunate to be able to learn from the generous women who contributed to this book.

Chapter Three

Hand Game Songs

OLD-FASHIONED AND MODERN HAND GAMES

In Oklahoma today, the hand game can be a recreational gambling game, often intertribal, or simply an enjoyable traditional activity with no money involved. The three Cheyenne songs in this chapter, while possibly still used in gambling sessions, are presented here as examples of "old-fashioned hand game" (nongambling) songs. Singers became nostalgic while discussing the activity. Mary Armstrong and her daughter Rena Rose Youngbear describe the differences between the old and new customs:

> MARY: You know the meaning of this hand game has been really changed, too. There was no money included, just effort to win. . . . [For my granddaughter's birthday] I said, "Well, let's have hand game, old-fashioned hand game!" [They said,] "OK, Grandma!" I said, "Well, I'm gonna bring my sticks out." So we played and we made all them guys lonesome because they remember their childhood when they used to play with them.

> RENA ROSE: [In old-fashioned hand game] when they had one session of hand game they had a drum in the center and they always sang round dances—or owl and rabbit— and they sang a song and the winners or the losers got up and danced and they always pledged food for the next game or they gave away for the birthday or the celebration they were having.

MARY: So that's what I'm saying, even our games changed, and we bet for our side, you know, and they come up with twenty dollars, or fifty dollars, and we got to match them. And the side that wins, money take all.

Mary's hand game sticks, which she made herself, are of willow. Her method: "Peel them when they're fresh and lay them where they can be straight when they dry out and just now you make a stick." Two kinds of sticks are used: sixteen short score-keeping sticks and two long pointing sticks. Eight short sticks and one pointing stick are of one color and used by one team; the opposition uses the remaining color-contrasting sticks. Mary's sticks are blue and red; in her set is an extra, unpainted replacement stick "in case someone gets careless and breaks one." She stores them in a long, thin calico bag with a drawstring. The remaining parts of the game are the "buttons" or "bones," four two-inch-long cylindrical beads, two of which are marked by a stripe in the middle and two left plain.

The scoring sticks are about a foot in length; the pointing sticks are longer by three inches or so. The pointing sticks are each tipped with a small, round "jingle" bell and two feathers attached by sinew thread. One of Mary's pointer sticks has magpie feathers, and the other has crow feathers. (The names of these two birds appear in the texts of two of the hand game songs in this chapter.) When used by the guesser in this hiding game, the team's stick is waved in the air in time with the music; the feathers shake around and the bell makes a soft jingle as the guesser determines where to point.

The object of the game is to locate the marked bead. On the guesser's opposing team, a person is chosen to hide the two beads, or "buttons," one in each hand. As the music is sung, the hider shakes the "buttons" around from side to side or from left to right. Natalie Curtis described hand game motions in the Cheyenne chapter of *The Indians' Book:* "The hands are often thrown out or crossed in the air, while mystic motions are made to confuse the guesser, or to blight his power of divination" (162). Songs are sung over and over until the bead is found, and sometimes continue even after a bead is found. Teasing motions of the feathers in the air are depicted in the texts of two of the hand game songs in this chapter.

When a guesser chooses, the feathered stick is used for pointing. For example, to indicate the left hand, the stick is held horizontally with feathers on the left side; the opposite indicates the right hand. A table on which the tally sticks are arranged and moved from one side to the other is the scoreboard. In old-fashioned hand game, these sticks simply lie on a table; in the modern gambling game, they stand perpendicular to the table in a rack so that the score can easily be seen by a larger group.

Hand game becomes more complicated when there are two hiders per team. If two people hide two sets of "buttons," the pointer has more guessing options; the pointer may guess:

1. left hand of one player
2. right hand of one player
3. both hiders' left hands
4. both hider's right hands
5. inside hands (from the perspective of four hands in a line)
6. outside hands

Guessing two people at once increases the hazard; two tally sticks can be gained or lost depending on accurate guesswork. A less risky move would be to guess about only one person; the result would be the winning or losing of only one point for the team. When pointing, the directions are shown by holding the stick as follows:

FIGURE 3

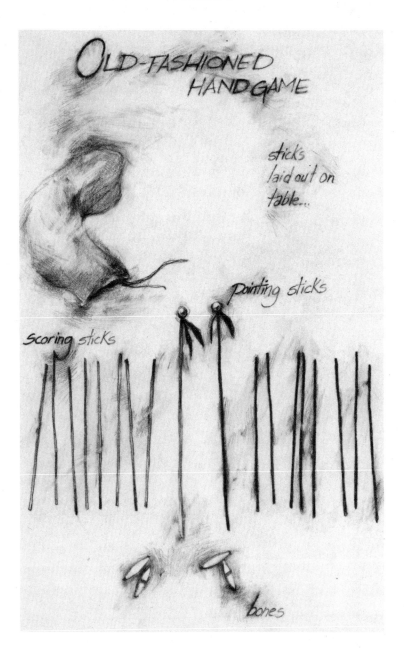

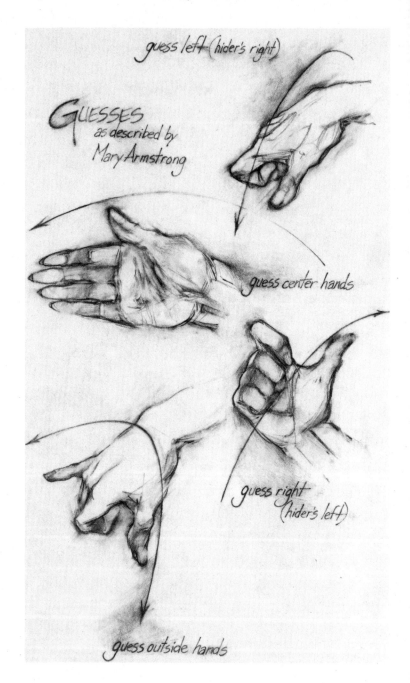

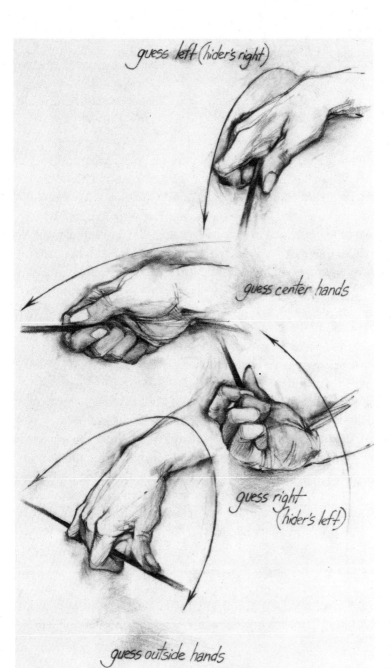

guess left (hider's right)

guess center hands

guess right
(hider's left)

guess outside hands

Left: stick perpendicular to arm, horizontal, feathers left
Right: same as above, feathers to right
Two lefts: same as left
Two rights: same as right
Inside: stick in line with arm, feathers pointing ahead
Outside: grasp middle of stick, perpendicular to arm,
              horizontal

Pointing can also be done without a stick, using the hand only. When the thumb points left, this indicates that the bead is hidden in the hider's left hand (or two hider's left hands). Guessers use the opposite sign to indicate right hand(s). When two hiders are playing, outside hands are indicated by the guesser's signal of a closed hand, palm down, with thumb and little finger extended (as in the letter *y* in American Sign Language, held on a horizontal plane.) Inside hands would be indicated by a flat open hand held vertically (thumb up). Sometimes the finder claps his or her hands before pointing.

In modern hand game, women often shake homemade rattles made from cans secured to the ends of dowels, then painted with bright colors and decorated with long fringes of yarn, plastic, or cellophane. The swish and flash of these hand game shakers is intended to keep up the team's spirits and to confuse the players of the opposing team. The hand game shakers are considered to be part of the modern hand game atmosphere. Although they add to the sound of the event, they are not considered to be musical instruments, but to function more like a cheerleader's pompon at a football game.

The songs in this chapter were sung in the homes Mary Armstrong of Geary, Oklahoma, and Bertha Little Coyote of Seiling. There was no drum present—in hand game, women do not play the drum anyway. Bertha Little Coyote simulated the beat of a drum on her kitchen tabletop to show how it would be played with the songs she sang. Bertha's tabletop

drum pattern (notated in quarter notes on a separate line below the song transcription) differs from the triple-meter dotted
rhythms often found in recorded examples of the Plains hand
games. This might indicate that the song, which sounds strictly
duple in meter, is quite old, preceding the modern, pantribal
gambling hand game style.

Number 12
"Crows and Magpies"
Bertha Little Coyote, 3/14/91

O   go gi o   o 5 -   Mo o i   ha ni i

Zo i   ha o no - ma no o - si yo ni vi vo zi hi

Zo i   ho o no - ma no o - si yo ni vi vo si hi.

Drum throughout
"Crows and Magpies"

Number 12
"Crows and Magpies,"
Bertha Little Coyote, 3/14/91

1. *As spoken*

O go gi̱ mo i ha ni̱
zo i ha o̱
ma no o si yo ni vi vo zi̱

2. *As sung*

O go **gi** o o
mo o i ha **ni** *hi*
zo i ha **o** *no*
ma no o si yo ni vi vo **zi** *hi*

3. *Translation*

O go gi̱	— crows
mo i ha ni̱	— magpies
zo i ha o̱	— they will fly
ma	— when
no o si yo	— hand game
ni vi vo zi̱	— modifies "hand game" to "hand-gaming"

4. *Free translation*

Crows and magpies will fly in when I'm hand-gaming!

Bertha Little Coyote sang "Crows and Magpies" (no. 12) slower than the usual tempo in order "to make the words and melody clear" for this preservation tape.

The song, intended to be repeated over and over until the hidden marked bead is found, consists of three phrases of irregular length (phrase 1: six beats; phrase 2: nine beats; phrase 3: six beats). The last phrase introduces a slight change from the preceding phrase; measure 8 differs from its corresponding measure 5 slightly (the pitch E is raised to an F). Otherwise, the two are similar enough to call them a pair of like phrases. Each phrase begins with the same rhythmic pattern, starts on the same pitch, and moves in the same initial melodic direction. The melody lies within the range of a fifth and, excluding the E in phrase 2, consists of four tones: D, F, G, and A.

An identifying feature of the American Indian hiding-game genre identified by Herzog and confirmed by the research of Densmore is the consistency of the repeated-phrase principle. "Crows and Magpies" is an exception to this principle owing to its single presentation of phrase 1. In this respect "Crows and Magpies" differs from the other hand game songs in this chapter.

The text of "Crows and Magpies" contains references that have meaning in two religious frameworks: the nineteenth century Ghost Dance and an older traditional Cheyenne creation story. The crow was the sacred bird of the Ghost Dance, regarded as the messenger of the spirit world, and by means of whose feathers one might be "borne upward to the spirit world" (Mooney 1896, 970). The Ghost Dance prophet Wovoka was referred to as "Crow"; Mo'ki, an Oklahoma Cheyenne woman who was a leader of the Ghost Dance movement, was referred to as "Crow Woman." The Cheyennes and Arapahos of Oklahoma developed a crow dance to be performed as a preliminary to the Ghost Dance ceremonies; it was "claimed by its inventors as a direct inspiration from the other world, where they saw it performed by 'crows,' or spirits of departed friends" (922). Crow designs appeared on Ghost Dance shirts, leggings, and moccasins, and dancers sometimes carried stuffed crows in the ceremony (982).

The magpie was another sacred bird of the Ghost Dance religion, "revered for [its] connection with the country of the messiah [Nevada, home of Wovoka] and the mythology of his tribe" (Mooney 1896, 982). The magpie was as sacred to the Paiutes as the eagle is to many American Indian tribes. "It bears a general resemblance to the crow or blackbird, being about the size of the latter, and jet black, with the exception of the breast, which is white, and a white spot on each wing. In its tail are two long feathers with beautiful changeable metallic luster" (998–99).

Both the crow and the magpie belong in another religious framework, playing important roles in a Cheyenne creation story. According to a story told by the tribal historian John Stands in Timber, the dominion of the earth and its resources were once the prize in a competition between a young man and the buffalo, who raced to determine who would be master. All the animals of the world except two ran with the buffalo. Only the crow and the magpie chose to run with the young man, and the magpie's swiftness brought about the victory for his team.

> The old men buffalo called this young man to come to them. "Well, you have won," they said. "From now on everything will be done by the outcome of this race. You are on top now, above every animal and everything in the world. All we animals can

do is supply the thing you will use from us—our meat and skins and bones. And we will teach you how to give a Sun Dance. . . . Since the magpie and crow were on man's side in the race they were treated with respect. They both eat buffalo flesh and other meat, and the Cheyennes are thankful to the magpie for her part in winning the race, so they do not kill her. (22–24)

There is a double appearance of crows and magpies in the hand game: the birds appear both in the text of the song "Crows and Magpies" and in the feathered accoutrements of the game. The crow and magpie feathers on the pointing sticks have their counterpart in the text: "Crows and magpies will fly in when I'm hand-gaming." Whether the song originally referred to the birds of Ghost Dance traditions or the young man's allies in the great race, it is certain that having such powerful birds fly in would bring power to the hand game player.

Number 13
"Crow"
Mary Armstrong, 9/18/91

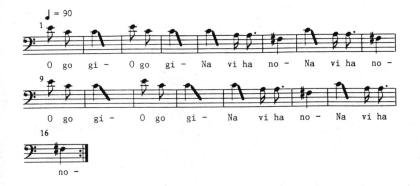

1. *As spoken*

O go gi
Na vi ha no
O go gi
Na vi ha no

2. *As Sung*

O go **gi,** O go **gi,**
Na vi ha **no,**
Na vi ha **no.**
(Repeat)

3. *Translation*

o go gi   — crow
na   — me, my, or I
vi ha no — flying around (vi) it (ha no)

4. *Free Translation*

Mary Armstrong:
Crow, crow,
I'm flying him around, I'm flying him
around!
(Repeat)

Mary Armstrong sang "Crow" (no. 13) in September 1990 at her home in Geary. Mary said that "Crow" in this song refers to the hand game pointing stick with crow feathers, and she waved the stick around in the air with rhythmic, jerky movements while singing. Mary said the song should be repeated until the bead is found.

The repeated-phrase principle identified by Herzog as characteristic of hiding-game songs is borne out in "Crow." Each phrase of the short song is repeated twice; the song is composed of two paired phrases. Like "Crows and Magpies," "Crow" begins with a descending major third. Four pitches are used in the melody: E, C, A, and F#. (In a Euro-American framework, this would spell a half-diminished seventh chord—not an easy group of pitches to sing.) The ends of the first paired phrases (last syllable of "o go gi") slide downward to an indeterminate level, indicated by a downward line from the initial pitch. This same effect appears on the first note of the second paired phrases on the syllable "na." All downward slides occur on the pitch C. The song contains a rhythmic pattern of paired two-beat units alternating with paired three beat units. These beat units reflect the motion of Mary's pointing stick; no accompanying drumbeat pattern was discussed.

The text—"Crow, crow, I'm flying him around, I'm flying

him around"—might in the past have referred to the hand-game button rather than a feathered pointing stick. Curtis observed hand-game hiding objects made of sticks "carved in the form of a little black bird, probably a crow, symbol of good" (161). Her description of Oklahoma Cheyenne hand-game at the turn of the century, there is no mention of pointing sticks with feathers.

A Cheyenne Ghost Dance song text that appears in Mooney's study is very similar to "Crow":

> A'gachi'hi,
> A'gachi'hi,
> I'nimä'iha',
> I'nimä'iha',
> Hi'tsina'yo,
> Hi'tsina'yo,
> Na'vishi'nima'yu'suwu'nutu',
> Na'vishi'nima'yu'suwu'nutu'.

Translation:

> The crow, the crow,
> He is circling around,
> He is circling around,
> His wing, his wing -
> I am dancing with it,
> I am dancing with it. (1896, 1034)

A distinctive feature of the visions received by Oklahoma Cheyenne and Arapaho Ghost Dancers was the element of play. Departed friends and relatives, sometimes engaged in playing games and gambling, appeared to dancers while in trances. Game accoutrements, with which Ghost Dancers hoped to inspire more visits with loved ones seen playing in the spirit world, were brought into the dance. Similar incidents incorporating gaming materials into Ghost Dance ceremonies have been identified among other Plains and Great Basin tribes. "The Pawnee, for instance, carried shinny balls or hoops in their dances and tried to induce visions with their aid; they also came to treat the hand game as a ceremony, its proper procedure being revealed in visions."[1]

Alexander Lesser comments on the next step in the historical process: "In the history of the Pawnee hand game we have the transformation of a gambling game into a complex ritual. As the doctrine which called these rituals into being weakens, the rituals tend to relapse once more into mere games" (330–31). According to Judith Vander, these comments apply also to Shoshone hand game and Ghost Dance songs: "Such human activities as dance and games can be either religious or social, depending upon the belief of the performers"(1986, 69).

Natalie Curtis's conclusion about hand games among Oklahoma Cheyenne people was that they were not religious ceremonies. The behaviors she observed, however, are replete with religious significance:

> The game opens with a prayer, delivered by the one who may be, for the night, the leader in the game. In some tribes the hand-game is itself a religious ceremony, but this is not the case among the Cheyennes. With the Cheyennes the details of the game may change with each night of the playing, so there is always a leader to direct the game. This leader has usually beheld in a dream the arrangement of the game—the placing of

---

1. Lowie, *Indians of the Plains,* 181. Cheyenne and Arapaho Ghost Dancers also sang about the women's game of "shinny," a ball game played with curved sticks and buckskin-covered buffalo hair ball; Cheyenne men played and sang gambling songs about throwing sticks through a rolling wheel (Mooney 1896, 964–65, 994).

the tally-sticks, and other details—for he has been taught by some spirit how the game is to be played on the night of his leadership, for, with the Indian, even sports are divinely directed. . . . The opening hand-game prayer asks that the game may be played as divinely revealed, and that to the people may be given happiness, good luck, health, welfare, and old age. With simple dignity, the leader tells of this dream, and gives his directions for the game. In making the preparations for the game, he accompanies his acts with the saying, "So was it seen by me," or, "So I heard it commanded," or, again, "According to the Spirit." (161)

Densmore's encounter with the hand game among Oklahoma Cheyennes led to the recording of three hand game songs from Elk Woman, who told Densmore that she got her hand game songs from inspiration received during fasting and praying. The evidence points to a strong relation between religious ceremony, especially the Ghost Dance, and the hand game among Cheyenne people.

Number 14
"Flying Around"
Mary Armstrong, Rena Rose Young Bear,
Mary Lou Blackbear, 9/18/91

Zi   do   ii   vi',   zi   do   ii   vi',   na   no   o   si

yo   o   ii   vi',   na   no   o   si   yo   o   ii   vi',

Number 15
"Flying Around" (Variant)
Bertha Little Coyote, 3/14/91

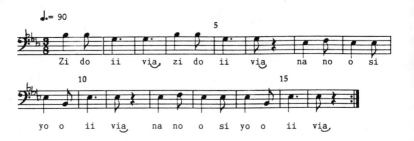

Zi   do   ii   via,   zi   do   ii   via,   na   no   o   si

yo   o   ii   via   na   no   o   si   yo   o   ii   via,

Drum throughout
"Flying Around

Numbers 14 and 15
"Flying Around,"
Mary Armstrong, Rena Rose Young Bear,
Mary Lou Birdshead Blackbear, 9/18/91
Bertha Little Coyote, 3/14/91

1. *As spoken*

Zi do ii via, zi do ii via,
Na no o si yo ii via *(repeat)*
Zi do ii via, zi do ii via,
Na no o si yo ii via *(repeat)*

2. *As sung (two versions)*

Mary, Rena, and Mary Lou:
Zi do ii vi', zi do ii vi',
Na no o si yo *o* ii vi'. *(repeat)*
Zi do ii vi', zi do ii vi',
Na no o si yo *o* ii vi. *(repeat)*

Bertha Little Coyote:
Zi do ii via, zi do ii via,
Na no o si yo *o* ii via *(repeat)*
Zi do ii via, zi do ii via,
Na no o si yo *o* ii via *(repeat)*

3. *Translation*

zi do	— this one (as opposed to "hi do"—this thing) According to Hart, "Zi do" indicates an animate object, whereas "hi do" indicates a thing. The bead within the hand takes on an animate quality as it "flies around."
ii via	— flying, flying around
na	— this, this thing, what (I'm hiding)
no o si yo	— hand game

4. *Free translation*

This one's flying around,
This one's flying around,
This hand game thing, this hiding thing,
is flying around!
This hand game thing, this hiding thing,
is flying around!

The first version of "Flying Around" (no. 14) was recorded in September 1990 in Geary by three women: Mary Armstrong, her daughter Rena Rose Young Bear, and Mary Lou Blackbear, an Arapaho married to a Cheyenne. The second version (no. 15) was recorded in March 1991 in Seiling; the singer is Bertha Little Coyote.

All singers concurred that "zi do" (this one) referred to the hidden marked hand game button. Bertha described her experience with hand game in the 1920s, explaining that the men and women would sing, and the men would play handheld drums. "Flying Around" is a song she remembers from that era: "That was our enjoyment. You make motions with your hands, back and forth, or however, and [the song is] saying, 'This button that I have in my hand is flying around, flying around, and . . . you're supposed to guess which hand I have it in.'" Like "Crows and Magpies" (no. 12), Bertha indicated how the drum beats would occur although she, as a woman, would not play the drum.

The two versions vary slightly at measure 7 (and corresponding measure 13 on the repeat of the phrase). Mary, Rena Rose, and Mary Lou sing a measure that is a repeat of the measure before; Bertha does not repeat, but sings one pitch on the same rhythmic figure. The pitch index of both versions consists of B flat, E flat, F, G flat, and the B flat an octave higher. The Euro-American ear is tempted to hear a fifth (dominant) relationship between the lower B flat and the final E flat; the melody moves from the initial B flat down to the central E flat in measure 5, with a dip to the lower B flat before the phrase ends on E flat. A rhythmic pattern of three beats per unit in the first paired phrases and five beats per unit in the second pair results in a beat pattern of 3, 3, 5, 5 for as long as the song is sung.

A fascinating aspect of these performances is that both the Geary women and Bertha sang the song with the same pitches, E flat and B flat being the most frequent. At the Geary session, Mary Armstrong's pitch was deferred to in all occasions of group singing; in Seiling, Bertha sang alone. Therefore, it was Mary's and Bertha's pitching of the song that matched up; they are the elders of the four women, and their memories for "old-fashioned" hand game go back the farthest.

Densmore noted that some Cheyenne and Arapaho singers had what she called "a sense of pitch level": "Singers with this sense of pitch level maintain the same pitch of keynote in long series of songs, even recording a song on the same pitch after a lapse of days or weeks" (109). Bertha's and Mary's pitch agreement could be attributed to aural memory resulting from years of hearing and singing the song. Another factor might be physiological memory of the song's placement in their vocal mechanism. Whether due to these factors, either singly or in combination, or to something else, the pitch agreement of these two singers is a remarkable phenomenon.

COMPARISON TO PREVIOUS FINDINGS

The three songs in this chapter are an interesting addition to hand game songs collected and investigated by Mooney, Densmore, and Herzog. The songs' texts are similar to those in Mooney's investigation. The three Cheyenne hand game songs in Densmore were sung by Elk Woman. Two have extreme differences from the songs here. No text was recalled by the singer. As opposed to the small ranges of the three songs in this chapter, the two wordless songs have ranges of an octave in one case and a ninth in the other. A third song, "Mad Bull's Hand Game Song," has three characteristics that are shared with the three songs in this chapter: dotted rhythms, a mix of two-and three-beat units, and melodic material composed of only three pitches within the range of a fourth.

Herzog outlined several characteristics of American Indian hiding-game songs, many of which also parallel Ghost Dance songs. The songs in this chapter display the following characteristics identified by Herzog: They are relatively fast in tempo and consist of short repeated phrases that contain a small number of tones. Their range is limited to a fifth. All three songs (and "Crow" in particular) exhibit characteristic "staccatos or rests and intakes of breath which are more frequent than physiologically necessary" (7). Rhythmic figures that after initial presentation characterize a song by their recurrence are found in all three examples.

By virtue of their text content, with references to the doctrine of the Ghost Dance and traditional pre-Ghost Dance creation stories, these songs seem to underscore further the connection between religion and everyday activity in the lives of Cheyenne people.

Chapter Four

War Songs

WAR MOTHERS AND WAR SONGS

Serving in the armed forces of the United States has provided the Cheyennes a means of demonstrating traditional courage, loyalty, and willingness to give up personal comfort for the good of the community. The centuries-old Cheyenne cultural necessity of proving one's bravery is fulfilled in modern battles, and men and women are honored today at powwows and dances for service to their country. Many Cheyennes have remarkable service records. At the Red Moon Powwow in 1991 I heard a reading of the service records of a single Cheyenne family, the Harts; it took forty-five minutes to list the military activities within this one highly respected family. To remember and pay homage to veterans and soldiers, groups such as the Oklahoma Inter-Tribal Veterans Auxiliary have been formed.

Led by Nellie (Hawk) Roman Nose, the auxiliary is headquartered in Kingfisher, Oklahoma. Nellie's group gathers to dance at benefit dances and other social dances held throughout Oklahoma. In this way, the group "helps out" the sponsoring family or organization by appearing at the dance, donating prizes for raffles, giving away to other members of the "head staff," and, by their physical presence, lending spiritual support to the dance. In hand-painted and fringed "club shawls" decorated with the auxiliary's insignia, the ladies, many of them elders, stand shoulder to shoulder to gourd dance. Sometime during the evening the auxiliary will do a "special."

During their special, the auxiliary leads a procession around the dance circle in slow measure to the beat of a veteran's song played by the center drum. Following the circular dance, the group lines up for a special gourd dance, and donations are placed at the feet of the elder leaders of the club. "Monetary gifts" are in turn presented by the auxiliary to the dance sponsors and various members of the head staff, along with other useful gifts such as blankets, linens, rugs, pillows, groceries, and shawls. The Oklahoma Inter-Tribal Veterans Auxiliary is only one of many organizations of this type (from various tribes) that can be found in Oklahoma. This type of club is also referred to as a "war mothers club," and as such is venerated in the community, and clubs are "called upon to help out" in instances where a show of support is needed.

The concept of "support" or "helping out" is another facet of Cheyenne cultural generosity. In this instance, "support" is provided in a spiritual as well as a material sense. Cheyenne valuing of the spiritual strength of women during arduous times is demonstrated in the war mothers clubs. This value, as well as the value of a warrior status among Cheyenne men, has long been a documented facet of Cheyenne culture, and the phenomenon has an accompanying musical component.

Songs to encourage bravery, commemorate war exploits, and express hope of safe return from battle are common among the Cheyenne songs documented in this century. The first transcriptions of Cheyenne music in 1882 (by Theodore Baker in *Über die Musik der Nordamerikanischen Wilden*) were war songs. The research of Natalie Curtis, Henry F. Gilbert, Frances Densmore, and Daniel Hodges contain notated war songs; George Bird Grinnell and Wayne Leman present war song texts.

Grinnell writes at length in *The Fighting Cheyennes* about the warrior ways of the Cheyenne people:

> After the question of providing subsistence for himself and his family, the main thing that occupied the mind of the Cheyenne was the protection of his people from the attacks of enemies and the effort to reduce the power of those enemies by attacks on them. The fighting spirit was encouraged. In no way could a young man gain so much credit as by the exhibition of courage. Boys and youths were trained to feel that the most important thing in life was to be brave; that death was not a thing to be avoided. (12)

The army of the United States found the Cheyennes an intrepid adversary in the nineteenth century; because of a desire for peace on both sides, the reservation period saw an end to the battles, but the warrior spirit of the Cheyenne people endures.

In the early twentieth century, many American Indians exhibited their customary courage in battle through active participation in World War I. Many volunteered for military service, and traditional war songs regained their function. When World War II broke out, Indian soldiers again participated, some playing vital roles as "code talkers," passing messages over battlefield communications radio in native languages that could not be interpreted by the enemy. The zealous activity of Native American soldiers in military service has been interpreted by William Powers as a reaffirmation of cultural institutions that were in decline:

> World Wars I and II, and to a lesser extent, the wars in Korea and Vietnam . . . gave American Indians the opportunity to reinforce

cultural institutions that might have become dysfunctional. Indian soldiers who participated were regarded as heroes by their people and, in accordance with tribal custom, were publicly acknowledged through songs, dances, and giveaways.(219)

At any powwow or social dance among Oklahoma Cheyenne people, dances in honor of veterans and soldiers are invariably requested by masters of ceremonies. Songs commemorating every American conflict from World War I to the Persian Gulf War have been made by singers. Dances to these songs are often led by men who bear wounds and disabilities acquired in wartime. Telling "war stories," in which brief incidents from battle experience are recalled, is a vital part of the sacred ceremonies of the Cheyenne people. Along with veterans' dances and war stories, war songs are a vital part of Cheyenne culture and can be sung by women or men.

This chapter contains two war songs, each of them an expression of the warrior ethos of Cheyenne people. Although alike in subject, they are different in mood, text, and sound. The first is an exhortation to a warrior; the second an exhortation to an enemy. One song is faster, but both are solemn.

Number 16
"Soldier Song"
Imogene Jones, Mary Lou Stone Road Prairie
Chief, Joan Swallow, 2/5/91

1. *As spoken*

Mo i hi ni stoo
Ni da va ni ga si vi o zi̱
Zi vi vo vo ni o zi̱
Ni dô mi̱ hi da niv.

2. *As sung*

Mo' o ni stoo, *i ya hi ya hi yo,*
Ni da vi ni ga si vi o **zi,** *yi*
Zi vi vo vo ni o **zi,** *ya hi yo,*
Ni dô **mi** hi da niv, *i yo hi yi yo hi yi.*

3. *Translation*

mo i hi	— elk
ni stoo	— whistling, howling, blowing horn
ni	— you
da va ni	— are going
ga si	— short
vi o zi̱	— journey (such as to war)
zi vi	— don't
vo vo ni o zi̱	— give up; surrender
ni	— you
dô mi̱	— are
hi da niv	— a man, mature

4. *Free translation:*

Whistling Elk,
You are going to war.
Don't surrender,
You are a mature man.

"Soldier Song" (no. 16) was recorded at the February 5, 1991, meeting of the Cheyenne and Arapaho Language Group; the singers are Imogene Jones, Mary Lou Stone Road Prairie Chief, and Joan Swallow. The song, said to be quite old, was reconstructed by the group, each of whom alone could not have sung the entire text and melody. One woman in the group (Jones) remembered the words to the last line but not the melody, while the others remembered the melody but were unsure of the last line of text. (For that reason, some singers drop out on the last line of the recording.) Thanks to the teamwork of Imogene Jones, Mary Lou Prairie Chief, and Joan Swallow, and some patient effort with the recording process, the different parts were combined into a complete song. The singers were pleased that the song could be reconstructed, because it was important to them that it not be forgotten.

The first words, "Mo i hi ni stoo" (Whistling Elk), form a proper name; the name of any young man can be inserted. The song's text encourages a young man preparing to go to war and perhaps leaving home for the first time. The line "ni dô mi̲ hi da niv" (you are a mature man) is further interpreted by Joan Swallow as "you are born a man." This reflects Grinnell's observation concerning the exhibition of courage in battle as a certain way to gain respect for a young warrior's manhood.

When sung, several words of the text are transformed from their spoken pronunciation. In the first line of sung text as it appears on the chart, "mo i hi" (elk) contains a vowel change, resulting in "mo' o" when sung. Three song words that end in voiceless vowels are also changed when sung: "vi o zi̲" to "vi o zi"; "vo vo ni o zi̲" to "vo vo ni o zi"; and "ni dô mi̲" to "ni dô mi."

Vocal stresses on the first of every group of two eighth notes throughout the song result in a lively performance with a strong feeling of duple meter. The number of beats per phrase follows the pattern 7, 6, 6, 8. Two rhythmic units, the quarter and eighth notes, predominate; in the third phrase is a quick syncopated pattern involving a sixteenth, an eighth, and a sixteenth rest on the word "zi vi' " (don't). The rhythmic coloring of "zi vi' " adds to the urgency of the message: "Don't surrender."

The melody contains seven pitches and begins and ends on the same note (C#), which is approximately central within the range of the song (a major ninth). A vocal challenge occurs in the third phrase on the word "vo vo ni o zi" (surrender; give up). On the syllables "ni o zi" the melody skips up an octave by using the stairstep of a third above the lower note. This is done in the time of two eighth notes—at a speed of 92 quarter notes per minute, a very quick leap. Like the aforementioned rhythmic device on "zi vi," the disjunct stairstep motive adds further expression to the song text, "zi vi vo vo ni o zi" (don't surrender). The phrase lying in the highest tessitura comes last, making the text line "ni dô mi hi da niv" (you are a mature man) have the effect of an affirmation of the song's hero. The message is aurally underscored with the strong vocables at the conclusion, a reprise of the song's repeated initial pitch.

Number 17
"War Song: God Is with Me"
Bertha Little Coyote, 3/13/91

hi   yi - a   ya   hi   yi,

10

a   hi   a   hi   yo - hi   yo - .

Chant

Ya -   hi   yi   a   ya   hi   yi,

a   i   yi -   a   ya   hi   yi,

A - -   hi   yi   a   ya   hi   yi,

hi   yi   a   a   ya   hi   yi,

15

a   hi   a   yi   o - hi   yo - .

Text

O -   da   khi -   ni   hi,

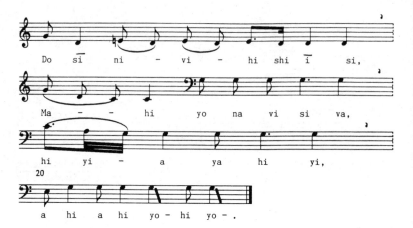

1. *As spoken*

Ma i̱ vi ho i̱,
Do sī ni mi hi shi ī si̱,
Ma hi yo na vi si vi vi̱.

O da khī ni̱,
Do sī ni mi hi shi ī si̱,
Ma hi yo na vi si vi vi̱.

2. *As Sung*

Chant:
Ya hi yi a ya hi yi,
A hi yi a ya hi yi,
A hi yi a ya hi yi,
Hi yi a ya hi yi,
A hi a yi yo hi yo.

Text:
Ma *i* vi ho*i,* *hi,*

Do sī ni mi hi shi ī *si,*
Ma hi yo na vi si vi (*va,*)
Hi yi a ya hi yi,
A hi a hi yo hi yo.

Chant:
(Repeat of vocables)

Text:
O da khī *ni, hi*
Do sī ni mi hi shi ī *si,*
Ma hi yo na vi si (*) *va*
Hi yi a ya hi yi
A hi a hi yo hi yo.

3. Translation

ma i	— red
vi ho	— white man
ma i vi ho	— red white man; German
do sī	— where
ni	— you
mi hi shi ī si	— run for life, seek refuge
Ma hi yo	— God
na	— me
vi si vi vi	— is there with
o da khī ni	— slit (eyes); Japanese

4. Free translation

German, where can you seek refuge?
God is with me.
Japanese, where can you seek refuge?
God is with me.

*"vi" left out by singer; see previous verse.

Interpretation by Bertha Little Coyote:
German, which way can you turn? Where
can you go?
God is with me.
Japanese, which way can you turn?
Where can you go?
God is with me.

"War Song: God Is with Me" (no. 17) was recorded on
March 13, 1991, in Seiling, Oklahoma. The singer, Bertha
Blackbeard Little Coyote, was born in 1912 in Canton, Oklahoma. "My Cheyenne name is E-no-ze, 'Sunset'," Bertha says,
and she explains that her name's deeper meaning refers to the
"end of the day when things are left behind." Therefore, her
Cheyenne name's translation would also be "Leaving Everything Behind." She is active in both Christian and Cheyenne
traditional forms of worship, and she enjoys talking about
God. A member of the editorial committee for David Graber's
Tsese-Ma' heone-Nemeotötse: Cheyenne Spiritual Songs, Bertha
contributed three Cheyenne hymns remembered from her childhood. A skilled beadworker, seamstress, homemaker, and grandmother, Bertha has represented the tribe in national meetings
of government agencies and the Mennonite Church, and in
1971 participated in the American Folklife Festival in Washington, D.C.

In her youth Bertha served in the armed forces, and later
she was instrumental in the establishment of the tribe's Community Health Representatives (CHR) program, organizing
carpools and driving tribe members to medical and other
health-related appointments. The most elderly of all the singers
in this book, she lives a busy life, enjoying many friends and

singing behind the drum at social dances and at the sun dance.[1]

Concerning "War Song: God Is with Me" Bertha stated: "I used to hear this song [during] World War I, and I also heard it in World War II. Of course, there are a number of songs that we're losing because we don't keep singing them . . . we're losing them. I'm sorry for that."

"War Song: God Is with Me" was recalled to Bertha's memory after she heard a song transcription from Densmore's *Cheyenne and Arapaho Music* played on an electronic keyboard. A woman Densmore identified as Woman Who Stands Aloof recorded "Song in Honor of a Successful Warrior" in Kingfisher, Oklahoma, in 1935. The rhythm of "Successful Warrior" is different from "God Is with Me," but the melodic similarity is unmistakable.

Densmore recorded no text or translation of the song in her monograph, and the accompanying narrative states that the "song has no words." The following notes by Densmore place the song in context: "When a war-party returned victorious, it was customary to find out who was first to take a scalp or to count coup. This having been determined, the mother or grandmother of the warrior sang in his honor. If neither of these relatives was present, an aunt or his wife might sing for him. Such a song is ['Song in Honor of a Successful Warrior']" (38).

Densmore ascertained in the melody of "Successful Warrior" a framework based on two descending fourths (E to B: A

---

1. Bertha and her sister Mary can be heard on the record *Seventeen Southern Cheyenne Songs,* recorded around 1969 and still available from Indian Records, Box 47, Fay, Oklahoma 73646. On the record, the ladies sing in support of Roy Nightwalker, Denny Old Crow, and Hailman Little Coyote on "War Dance," "Round Dance," "Scalp Dance," and "49 Social Songs."

to E) and featuring two pitches one whole tone above the lower pitches of the two fourths (i.e., C sharp and F sharp). This framework she considered to be peculiar in the light of what she labeled as the "pure major" and "pure minor" tonalities of songs of other Cheyenne war songs she had collected.

The melody framework of Bertha's "War Song" is similar to that of "Successful Warrior." The text section beginning at measure 6 has a descending fourth followed by a major second (F sharp to C sharp; followed by D sharp); at measure 8 the melody shifts to a lower range by means of a descending fourth from B to F sharp. A G sharp appears in measure 9 between B and F sharp. The shared melodic material between the two songs makes them recognizably similar.

When I first began to study this song, I was struck by what seemed to be a melodic difference between the portions containing the words "ma i̱ vi ho i̱" (German) and "o da khī ni̱" (Japanese). The melodies seemed to be slightly different at these parallel phrases, and to my ear were particularly interesting and appealing. I decided to ask Bertha more about this song, and had a chance when I saw her a few months later at a powwow. We enjoyed a dinner of stew and frybread together, and then we discussed singing.

"Bertha, do you remember this?" I asked, then sang "War Song" for her, trying to copy her vocal style and render the Cheyenne words as accurately as I could. Teasing wrinkles appeared around Bertha's eyes as she said, "It sounds like you're trying to sing that song." She then listened carefully and corrected me as I sang a minor second on "O da khī ni̱." Bertha said that the melody that went with "Ma i̱ vi ho i̱" should be the same when singing "O da khī ni̱." When I told her that I was trying hard to sing it just the way she did, Bertha told me that the pronunciation of the Cheyenne long ī sound (an unfamiliar sound to a non-Cheyenne speaker) was causing

me to *hear* the third syllable of "O da khī ni" as different from
what it actually was. Once again, I was struck by Bertha's
sophisticated musical expertise and her ability not only to hear
my error but also to correct it and explain the music theory
behind the problem.

It is precisely this kind of musical expertise that demands
that the chosen terminology of the singers themselves be used
by anyone attempting to analyze and discuss Cheyenne music.
The opening vocable refrain of "War Song" has been labeled
"chant," and the portions that contain translatable Cheyenne
words are labeled "text." Singer/consultants for this project
often referred to vocable sections of songs as "chant." "Chant"
in this context should not be misconstrued as having similarity
to Gregorian chant, playground chants, or even sea chanteys.
Songs in this book are annotated using Cheyenne terminology
at every opportunity, with no reference intended to definitions
of the same words within other musical systems.

In "God Is with Me," two chant sections alternate with two
text sections. At first, corresponding notated sections do not
appear to be in the same tone system; chant section 1 has been
transcribed one half step higher than the remaining three sections. Comments on "God Is with Me" are based on the assumption that tonal inconsistency between sections does not
preclude comparison of corresponding song sections as if they
were uniform in pitch inventory. The pitch of the recorded song
begins to drop midway through measure 3 (see bracketed section indicating lowering of pitch), descending downward until
measure 5, when it settles a whole step lower than the opening.
The pitch ambitus that begins at measure 6 is retained until the
second chant section, which lies a half step higher.

The range of "War Song: God Is with Me" is unusually wide:
an octave and a fifth. Both text sections and the second chant
section begin on the same (relative) pitch (G) and end one

octave lower. The first chant section begins on a rising fourth, the second note of which is one octave higher than the last pitch of the section. The initial interval functions as an introduction to the song, and the effect is not repeated.

The tempo of "God Is with Me" is slower than "Soldier Song"; the text deals with a serious matter to Cheyenne people. Discussion of this song text with Lenora Hart revealed that within the words "Do sī ni mi hi shi ī si̱" (literally, "where you would run for life [or seek refuge]") is the implication that the enemy's biggest problem is not physical but spiritual. The adversary's lack of spirituality and therefore the possibility of succor from a force that transcends the physical realm is implicit in the text of the song. To a Cheyenne, to be without help from "Ma hi yo" (God) would be intolerable; his presence is invoked in every situation of life, whether it be the holiest annual ceremony or the small events of every day. To proclaim "Ma hi yo na vi si vi vi̱" (God is with me) is to renew in oneself the benevolent spirit that has superior knowledge of the workings of the cosmos. The implication of such a belief is that the enemy, who has no such sacred connection, is therefore powerless. The enemy is without "support," with no one to "help out."

OTHER OBSERVATIONS ON WAR SONGS

War songs, especially those sung by men, have been available for study in relative abundance compared to other genres in Plains music. In his comments concerning melodies of many songs of Plains tribes, Bruno Nettl points out what he calls a "terrace-type" movement:

> Melodies show the following phrase pattern: each phrase descends, and each begins somewhat lower than the previous one. Towards the end of a song the phrases do not usually descend as much as at the beginning, but they tend to flatten

out, as it were, the last phrase lingering on the final, lowest pitch for several notes . . . This type of melodic movement as a whole is called "terrace-type" because of its visual resemblance to terraces in this graphic expression. (1953, 25).

In some ways, Bertha Little Coyote's "War Song: God Is with Me" demonstrates terrace movement. Using the second text portion as an example, the high G descends by a fourth to D, then to the G below, lingering on or close to the lower G for the two final phrases. The song differs from the terrace pattern in that each phrase does not start lower than the phrase before; there is instead a pattern of two paired similar phrases followed by the "flattened-out" last phrase. The return to a high pitch level in each section gives the effect of terraced strophes. According to Nettl, strophic forms are another Plains song characteristic.

The disjunct songs in this chapter fit Nettl's perceived model of "uneven distribution of tones within the octave. A typical uneven construction . . . is: tonic, perfect fourth, perfect fifth, major sixth, perfect octave, minor ninth (all reckoned from the tonic)" (1953, 29). The issue of which note is tonic is a debatable one; for the purposes of comparison to Nettl's model, an aural sensation of relative melodic stability seems to indicate F sharp as a tonic possibility in "Soldier Song." (With the exception of a single E, F sharp is also the lowest note of the song.) From F sharp the interval distribution contains a major second, perfect fifth, major sixth, minor seventh, and octave. The interval distribution of "War Song: God Is with Me" has been reckoned from G and contains a major second, perfect fourth, perfect fifth, major sixth, and octave. "Soldier Song" contains three and "War Song: God Is with Me" contains four out of the six intervals of Nettl's typical distribution. Although the songs do not perfectly fit the model, the two songs do not contain much stepwise motion and are melodically disjunct.

The vocal style contrasts between the two war songs in this chapter are marked. "Soldier Song" is almost strident, with no vibrato, but instead, a pulsation on the longer notes of the song. This pulsation, as well as the tension and urgent quality of the vocal style, resembles that described by Nettl as characteristic of Plains music. Of all the songs collected here, the performance of "Soldier Song" stands out in its resemblance to the sound of the predominantly male drum.

Bertha Little Coyote's war song is quite different in vocal style. Although quietly intense, it is not strident, and the disjunct melody is sung in a smooth, connected fashion. Bertha's performance of this war song, as well as that of her other songs on the tape, demonstrate a characteristic observed by Densmore: "The Cheyenne . . . according to these phonograph records, have a custom of phrasing their melodies without the use of rests [demonstrating] an ability to sing long phrases without taking breath" (108). The phrases of Bertha's songs are quite long and her pauses for breath are smooth and controlled, another demonstration of her skill as a singer. (Bertha is proud of one of her nicknames: "Dinah Shore.")

Two statements by Natalie Curtis concerning Indian warfare sum up the character of the two war songs in this chapter. "Soldier Song," with its exhortation "ni dô mi hi da niv" (you are a man), exemplifies the principle that "the war-path was most often the path of individual adventure" (154). "War Song: God Is With Me" illustrates the character of many victory songs, speaking of "the profound belief that great deeds are achieved through a power that is greater than man" (155).

It is important to remember that, in Cheyenne culture both as chronicled in the nineteenth century and as witnessed today, warriors are not always male. From Calf Road Woman (the girl who saved her brother) to the young women in the present-day military, we see evidence of ongoing female involvement in the business of doing battle. Bertha Little Coyote, eighty-one years old and herself a veteran, is like a time bridge between the buckskin-clad horsewomen of an earlier era and those today who wear camouflage fatigues and fight under the same flag that Black Kettle waved in vain.

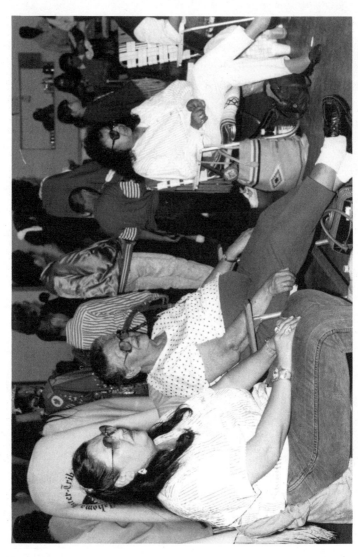

Rena Rose Youngbear and Mary Armstrong sit behind the drum and sing at a benefit dance. The dancers circling behind are doing a war dance. (Mary Jo Ruggles)

Nellie Hawk Roman Nose leads her war mothers club in a war dance around the drum (1991). The author dances in the rear. (Mary Jo Ruggles)

Nellie Hawk Roman Nose's club, the Oklahoma Inter-Tribal Veterans Auxiliary, stands in a row to gourd dance (1991). (Mary Jo Ruggles)

Diane and Burton Hawk examine some valuable tribal records. Without the help of these two, this book would not have been possible. (Photo by Virginia Giglio)

June Warden Black at a benefit dance, 1991. (Mary Jo Ruggles)

Bertha Little Coyote, my dear friend, 1993. (Mary Jo Ruggles)

Mary Lou Birdshead Blackbear, a fine singer and bingo player. (Mary Jo Ruggles)

Wilma Blackowl Hamilton and her grandson Gray Eyes, 1991. (Mary Jo Ruggles)

The Hawks' camp at a traditional Cheyenne event, summer 1991. Note the willow shade juxtaposed with twentieth-century tarpaulins. Dried meat is hanging inside the tipi. (Mary Jo Ruggles)

Chapter Five

Social Songs

GIVING AWAY, COURTING, AND FLIRTING

Cheyenne people are devout and home-loving, and their cultural pride and remarkable resiliency have helped them to withstand considerable hardships. They are also a laughing and weeping people, as the songs in this chapter demonstrate. A solemn song is juxtaposed with a teasing song; these in turn are followed by variants of a song that is considered somewhat risqué. The first two are possibly the oldest of all the songs in this book and, according to the singer, are seldom heard anymore. The last song—the funny one—is well known among today's Oklahoma Cheyennes.

What kinds of things do modern Cheyenne people do for fun? Many men and women enjoy craftwork such as beading, painting, sewing, and leather and feather work. They enjoy bowling, watching football games, going to rodeos, raising pets, playing bingo, and sitting in front of the television. A considerable number of Oklahoma Cheyennes participate regularly in social dances and in the giveaways that accompany those activities.

As described in chapter 1, giving is a vital part of Cheyenne life. Giveaway ceremonies occur at many events: major ceremonials, funerals, social dances, and powwows. Gift giving on a less formal basis is constant among Cheyennes, with the thoughtfulness, usefulness, or appropriateness of a gift appreciated above the cost. Larger, more formal giveaways may cost the givers much money, sometimes sacrificially so. Today as in past times, some of the most valuable and appreciated gifts are horses, tents, rifles, and thick colorful woolen blankets such as those manufactured by the venerable Pendleton Company of Oregon.[1] Not only are such gifts prized for their beauty and value, but they symbolize the glory of prereservation Cheyenne history.

1. Pendleton blankets not only are costly (about $120 apiece) but also increase in value with time. Some are sold to collectors as antiques, and some are used by high-fashion manufacturers to make expensive jackets and full-length coats.

Number 18
"Giveaway Song"
Bertha Little Coyote, 3/14/91

45

I - si ho dova ni ta - no hi yi ho vi

50

yo hi yi, O - va nii sto, va nii -

55 60

sto na ni, i ho do va na do vi yo hi yi

Chant 65

yoy. I ya hi ya a ya hi yi ho vi

70

yo hi yi, I ya hi ya hi ya hi yo,

75

I ya hi ya hi ya hi yo i yi ho vi

80

yo hi yi yi, I ya hi ya hi ya

hi hi yi,   A hi   ya hi ya   i ya   ho   vi yo

hi   yi   yoy.   O –   va hi   ha   si – sto

vi   yo   hi   yi,   Ho –   vī hi   hi   yi

hi   yi,   I –   si   ho   dova   nī   tan,   o

hi   yi ho   vi   yo   hi   yi,   O –   va nii

sto, va   nii –   sto na   ni,   I   ho do   va na

do   vi   yo   hi   yi   yo – .

1. *As spoken*

O va hi
si sto vi ho vī hi
i sī ho do va nī ta ni̠
o va nii hii sto ve̠ na ni
i ho do va na do̠

2. *As sung*

Chant:
I ya hi ya,
Hi ya hi yi
O vi yo hi yi,
I ya hi ya
I ya hi yo,
I ya hi yi a ya
Hi yo hi yi
Ho vi yo hi yi,
I ya hi yo
I ya hi hi ya,
A hi yo hi ya hi yi
O vi o hi yoy.

Text:
O va hi *ha,*
Si sto vi, *yo hi yi,*
Ho vī hi *hi yi hi yi,*
I sī ho do va nī ta **no** *hi yi,*
Ho vi yo hi yi,
O va nii sto, va nii sto na ni,*I ho do va
ni do
Vi yo hi yi yoy.
Chant:
I ya hi ya,
A ya hi yi
Ho vi yo hi yi,

*The line "nii sto, va nii sto na ni" is a combination of "nii hii sto vǝ" (death; dying) and "na ni" (our). See also the corresponding line in the second text section.

I ya hi ya
Hi ya hi yo,
I ya hi ya hi ya
I yo hi yi
Ho vi yo hi yi yi,
I ya hi ya,
Hi ya hi hi yi,
A hi ya hi ya i yi
Ho vi yo hi yi yoy.

Text:
O va hi *ha,*
Si sto vi, *yo hi yi,*
Ho vī hi *hi yi hi yi,*
I sī ho do va nī tan, *o hi yi,*
Ho vi yo hi yi,
O va nii sto, va nii sto na ni,
I ho do va ni do
Vi yo hi yi yo.

3. Translation

o va hi	— all on earth; my fellow men
si sto vi	— things
ho vī hi	— nothing
i sī	— it is
ho do va ni ta ni̱	— not difficult
o va	— except
nii hii sto ve̱	— death; dying
na ni	— our
i ho do	— it is
va na do̱	— difficult

4. *Free translation*

Bertha Little Coyote: "My fellow men,
there is nothing that can cause hardship
or is difficult as death. It's the hardest
part of life."

"Giveaway Song" was sung by Bertha Little Coyote in Seiling, Oklahoma, on March 14, 1991. The memory of this song
was triggered when she heard the text of "Old War Song" from
Frances Densmore's monograph (35); Densmore's source was
Elk Woman, who sang the song in 1935. The translation of Elk
Woman's song was "The stones are all that last long."[2] Densmore's transcription of the melody of the song does not resemble the melody of Bertha's song, but the brief yet eloquent text
brought the "Giveaway Song" to her mind. Bertha said the
words mean:

"My fellow men, there is nothing that can cause hardship or is
difficult as death. [Death] is the hardest part of life." And in
Indian, in Cheyenne, trying to interpret what I'm trying to say in
my native language, which is Cheyenne, sometimes I cannot
find an English word to fully describe the Indian words that are
put in this song. But it means, anything is replaceable, but death
is hard to take. You don't see that person here on earth any-

2. Bertha remembered the existence of another song with a text much like that
of Elk Woman's, but could not recall the melody or all the words. Bertha's
interpretation of the word "stones" is "mountains"; this change would transform
the English text to "Only the mountains live long." This resembles the text of
the famous death song sung by White Antelope while standing before the
attacking soldiers at Sand Creek: "Nothing lives long, only the earth and the
mountains" (Hyde, *A Life of George Bent,* 155; Grinnell, *Fighting Cheyennes,*
178). Powell identifies a song with the text "My friends, nothing lives long,
except the rocks!" as a song of the Kit Fox, one of the clans of the Cheyennes
(*Sweet Medicine* 1:351).

more. And that's a giveaway song [sung] if they have things to give. A lot of times they would give away horses, blankets, material things, and they sang this song. They never expected anything returned.

One type of giveaway occasion that fits the text of Bertha's song is the Cheyenne funeral. Cheyennes demonstrate their value of life above material things by a considerable show of generosity at ceremonies in honor of the dead. When someone dies, many gifts are given by the family of the deceased to those who come to the funeral. One old Cheyenne custom is for a wife to give away all the goods in the house in honor of her deceased husband. The custom is still adhered to by some Oklahoma Cheyennes.

After the funeral, the family refrains from participating in dances, powwows, or other social activities until a period of mourning has passed (approximately one year). The official end of mourning is achieved at a family-sponsored memorial dance in honor of the deceased; at this time the faces of family members are painted with ceremonial designs that symbolically wipe away their tears and put smiles back on their faces. Individual family members are "smoked off" when an elder fans cedar or sweet grass smoke up and down and around them. Speeches are made (sometimes by an honorary "family spokesman") and prayers prayed for the visitors on behalf of the family. Afterward, a family giveaway takes place and a large dinner is served to all present. After the painting ceremony, memorial songs are sung by the drum, and the whole company enjoys an evening of social dancing and visiting with old friends. Money received during the evening from raffles, auctions, and donations from dancers help defray the costs of the memorial dance.

The Cheyenne customs of mourning and of giveaways are very old, as is the "Giveaway Song." Bertha stated that she never hears the song anymore, and it was difficult for Lenora

Hart to provide a word-for-word translation of the song. One distraction during the translation of the song was the presence of individual syllables of definable words in the vocable chant portions of the song. These syllables, which seem to have broken loose from their mother words, also appear among the vocables that are interspersed between lines of text.

There are four sections of the song as Bertha performed it, with chant (vocable refrain) sections alternating with text sections. Vocables that resemble Cheyenne words or portions of words are "hi" and, in combination, "o vī" and "ho vī." "O vī" and "ho vī" resemble portions of the words "o va hi" (my fellow men), "si sto vi" (things), "ho vi hi" (nothing), and "o va" (except). "Hi," a common vocable, is also in this case the ending syllable of two text words: "o va hi" (my fellow men) and "ho vī hi" (nothing). The vocables of this old song might support the theory that some American Indian vocables, rather than existing as meaningless discrete entities, might have originated as complete words, or might have been words changed on the basis of poetic license to fit a melody or a rhythm.[3]

An example of such an adjustment occurs in the sixth line of text on "nii sto, va nii sto na ni." As pointed out in the note to the text, the words are a combination of "nii hii sto və̀" (death, dying) and "na ni" (our). The combination of the two when singing results in an entirely different set of syllables; someday these might be interpreted as vocables if no one remembers how the sounds were put together.

Because Bertha Little Coyote is considered to be a fine singer, her vocal style can serve as a clue to traditional performance

3. The Cherokee ethnomusicologist Charlotte Heth has outlined various ideas about vocables in American Indian music (1975, 117–29). Vocables might be as important to the identity of a song as its melody; in some cases, vocable syllables might convey as much meaning to the singer as full words.

practice. Chant sections of "Giveaway Song" are not uniform; there are variations between sections in rhythm, melody, and vocables. The general musical sense, however, is similar enough to make the song identifiable from its chant no matter which version is heard. The variations point out that the chant is not strict, but follows loosely the same melodic, rhythmic, and vocable patterns; these vary, perhaps, according to the prerogative of the singer or the context of the performance. Interesting questions arise concerning the musical reasons behind the differences. Some considerations are: (1) the vicissitudes of memory; (2) a desire for variety or other aesthetic choices; (3) breath control or other physiological factors; (4) stylistic tradition, learned through emulation of good singers and practiced by vocal experimentation, either consciously or unconsciously.

The range of "Giveaway Song" is quite wide, an octave and a fourth. Bertha's voice shifts easily into each new vocal placement. The rhythm of the song is complex and shifting; the song has been transcribed in small units of three to five eighth notes, though overall pulse, is slow and nonmetric.

Bertha's next song contrasts with the solemn "Giveaway Song." "Sweetheart Song" (no. 19) carries a flirtatious message between a young man and a young woman. Bertha said: "That's an old song. That's a girl trying to get her sweetheart to be jealous of her. She's telling him she was going to get married, and he says, 'I don't care, go ahead and have four husbands if you want.'"[4]

---

4. This could have been a more severe insult than it appears to be. According to Llewellyn and Hoebel, "evidence makes it clear that a woman who has been divorced four times became any man's bait" (*The Cheyenne Way*, 210).

Number 19
"Sweetheart Song"
Bertha Little Coyote, 3/13/91

hum – mi – a   hi   yi o   hi   ya

hi   yi,   Vo – – zi   vi   ni   vi

hi   ma   zi   ya   hiya.

Chant

I   ha   i   ya   hi   yi   a   hi

ya   o   i   ya   hi   yi,

hi   ya   i   ya   hi   yi   a   hi

i   ya   hi   yi   Ya   hi   i   ya

i   yi   a   hi   yi   o   hi   ya

1. *As Spoken*

Nī mi o o̧, hi no vi dī no o̧
na doo sii hi hum mi̧
voo zi̧ vī ni vi hi ma zi̧.

2. As sung

Chant:

I ya hi ya
hi yi a hi i ya hi yi,
A hi ya ya o hi yi
A hi yi o
O hi yo hi yi,
Yo hi yo hi yi
A hi ya ho o i yo hi.

Text:

Nī mi *i o o,* hi no vi dī no *o,*
Na doo si hum mi* *a hi yi o*
Hi ya hi yi,
Voo *zi* vī
Ni vi hī ma *zi ya hi ya.*

Chant:

I ya hi ya
hi yi a hi
ya o i ya hi yi,
I ya hi ya
hi yi a hi
i ya hi yi,
ya hi i ya i yi
A hi yi o hi ya hi yi,
Yo i ya hi yi a hi
yo o i ya hi
i yo hi yoy.

---

*This line of text ("Na doo si hum mi") is formed from an elision of the words "Na doo sīī" and "hi hum mi."

Text:
Nī mi *i o o,* hi no vi dī no *o,*
Na doo si hum mi *a hi yi o*
Hi ya hi yi,
Voo *zi* vī
Ni vi hī ma *zi ya hi yi.*

3. Translation

nī mi o ǫ	— sweetheart; boy- or girlfriend
hi no vi dī no ǫ	— be brave; have courage
na	— I
na doo sĩĩ	— I am going
hi hum mị	— get married
voo zị vi	— even though
ni vi	— four
hī ma zị	— spouses; husbands

4. Free translation

Sweetheart, take courage,
I'm going to marry you even though
you're my fourth man.

Bertha Little Coyote: "I don't care, go
ahead and have four husbands if you
want."

Lenora Hart adds another interpretation of the song: "Sweetheart, take courage, I'm going to marry you even though you're
my fourth man." Themes of multiple spouses and jealousy run
through several popular intertribal social songs among Okla-

homa Indians. For example, the inter-tribal Forty-Nine song "Sixteen Times" has an English text that is reminiscent of Lenora Hart's interpretation of "Sweetheart Song":

> Oh, yes I love you honey, dear,
> I don't care if you marry sixteen times,
> I'll get you yet.

Another popular Forty-Nine song is "Blackjack Daisy":

> Blackjack Daisy,
> she got mad at me
> because I said hello to my old-timer,
> but that's just OK with me.

"Sweetheart Song" song was recalled to Bertha's memory by the text and melody of "I Am Going to Marry Another Man" from Densmore's collection. It was sung by Woman Who Stands Aloof, identified by Densmore as the wife of Bob-Tail Wolf. The text is a dialogue:

WOMAN: "My sweetheart, don't take it too hard, what I am going to say, I am going to get married."
MAN: "You can have two [husbands, for all I care]."

Densmore writes:

Frustration appears in ["I am Going to Marry Another Man"]. A young man and a young woman had been sweethearts for a long time, but she decided to marry someone else. It became necessary to make this known to the young man. She broke the news with hesitation but he replied that he had no feeling in the matter. This is expressed in the words of the song and the form of the melody. Six intervals of a fourth characterize the opening measures. This is an awkward interval, and is followed by a repetition of the tones A and G, these in turn being followed by a quarter rest. The closing phrase expresses a gay indifference. (104)

Densmore's transcription contains no chant section; she does not indicate whether a chant or vocable refrain alternated with text sections as is the case in Bertha Little Coyote's "Sweetheart Song."

The rhythm of the two songs is quite different. Densmore's transcription contains regular measures of two or three beats each. The rhythm of "Sweetheart Song" is more elusive; the phrases are long, and in this case, breath marks between phrases in the transcription indicate spaces of brief but irregular length. The song seems to be sung to accommodate breathing at will rather than with the goal of adjusting breathing to the phrasing of the song.

The text sections of "Sweetheart Song" differ in rhythm from the Densmore song, but the same basic melodic shape is present. Bertha's song reiterates the intervals of a fourth that Densmore found remarkable. The melody on the words "na doo si hum mi" ("I am going to get married"), however, descends and is conjunct, whereas most of the Densmore song contains disjunct intervals. The range in both songs is the same: one octave plus a fourth. Bertha's song begins and ends on C, as does the other song; this may be due to a pitch having been established in her memory by electronic keyboard while listening to a brief play-through of songs in the collection. It is also possible that the song has been established at a concrete pitch level in her aural memory, a phenomenon that already been noted in the case of the hand game song "Flying Around."

Number 20
Forty-Nine Song: "Ma ta Gi sso,"
Mary Armstrong, Rena Rose Young Bear,
Mary Lou Birdshead Blackbear, 9/18/91

Ma ta   gi - sso, ma ta   gi - sso, hi yi   ya   hi   ya,

Szi vi   do do   khi   mo - vo,   hi   ya hi   yo, Na do ssi

vi ssto mo - a   hi   ya ho vi   ya hi - ya hi yoy.

Number 21
"Ma ta Gi sso" (Variant),
Mary Armstrong, 9/18/90

Ma ta   gi - sso, ma ta   gi - sso, hi yi   ya   hi   ya,

Svi vi   do do   khi   mo - vo,   hi   ya hi   yo, Na do ssi

vi ssto mo - a   hi   ya ho vi   ya hi - ya hi yoy.

Number 22
"Ma ta Gi sso" (Variant),
Rena Rose Young Bear, 9/18/90

Ma ta gi - sso, ma ta gi - sso, hi yi ya hi
ya, Szi vi do do khi mo - vo hi ya hi yo, Na
do ssi vi ssto mo - a hi ya ho vi ya hi - ya
hi yoy.

Numbers 20–22
Forty-Nine Song: "Ma ta Gi sso"
Mary Armstrong, Rena Rose Young Bear,
Mary Lou Birdshead Blackbear, 9/18/90

1. *As spoken*

Ma ta gi sso, ma ta gi sso,
Szi vi do do khi̱ mo vo̱,
Na do ssi̱ vi ssto͠o mo̱.

2. *As sung*

Ma ta gi sso, ma ta gi sso,
hi yi ya hi ya,
Szi vi do do **khi** mo **vo,**
hi ya hi yo,
Na do **ssi** vi ssto **mo**
A hi ya ho
vi ya hi ya hi yoy.

3. *Translation*

ma ta	— wild; crazy; loose
gi sso	— diminutive; little
ma ta gi sso	— wild girl; crazy girl
szi vi	— don't
do do khi̱	— talk about
mo vo̱	— her
na	— I
na do ssi	— I will
vi ssto͠o mo̱	— marry, to be with

4. *Free translation*

Crazy girl, crazy girl,
Don't talk about her.
I am going to marry her.

"Ma ta Gi sso" ("Crazy Girl") (nos. 20–22) is a well-known song among Oklahoma Cheyennes; it is probably sung along with car or truck cassette players as much as it is sung at Forty-Nine dances. (See chapter 1 for a description of Forty-Nine dances.) Cassette tapes of Forty-Nine songs with both American Indian–language and English lyrics can be purchased at powwows, Indian craft stores, and through mail order from the growing number of Native American music outlets. A version of "Ma ta Gi sso" appears on the tape *"49" Volume One* from Indian Sounds; on the cassette the song is labeled "Cheyenne Song."

The commercial cassette version of "Cheyenne Song" includes vocable refrain sections alternating with text sections; the version sung by Mary Armstrong, Rena Rose Young Bear, and Mary Lou Birdshead Blackbear for this book contains no vocable refrain or chant. When singing for fun away from the Forty-Nine dance, chant might not be a necessary component.

The event that has come to be called "Forty-Nine" is said to have originated among the Kiowas, another Oklahoma tribe. The noun *Forty-Nine* is the name of a dance, but the word can also be a verb ("to Forty-Nine" is to participate in a Forty-Nine). Participants are called "Forty-Niners," as are the dances and songs sung. Various stories are told about the etymology of Forty-Nine. Some say that the name recalls a time when fifty warriors went out and only forty-nine returned; some say fifty went out and only one returned, the remaining forty-nine having lost their lives in battle. Another source suggests that

"Forty-Nine" was an inside joke among Indians in a Wild West show, amused by the barker's cry, "See forty-nine dancing girls! Forty-nine!" Others have said that the tradition of "Forty-Nining" began in 1849, when war dances were held all night to keep enemy soldiers awake. Still others point to 1949, when after World War II Native American soldiers were welcomed home with war songs. Considering all of the word's possible roots and meanings, it is no wonder that people smile when they hear the number forty-nine, and sometimes the exclamation "Party time!" is heard when the number is called at bingo games in Cheyenne country.[5]

The "party" referred to by the bingo players is a moonlit nighttime dance, generally held after a powwow, lasting until sunrise. According to Mary Armstrong, these dances were originally sponsored by parents who wanted to introduce their adolescent sons or daughters to other friends their age. Food was provided, and songs and dances included family members of all ages. Unfortunately, many modern Forty-Nines have degenerated into occasions of excessive drinking, often accompanied by fights. In Oklahoma, Forty-Nines are also targets for racist attacks by non-Indians; drive-by shootings have occurred, and some people have been seriously injured.

For these reasons, Forty-Nine dances have lost their appeal for many, but the songs continue to be enjoyed. The Forty-Nine repertoire is another facet of the pan-Indian phenomenon; songs are shared freely between tribes at intertribal events, and some songs are heard all over the continent. Some of the old songs were originally war journey songs, much like "Soldier Song" in chapter 4. Another source of Forty-Nine songs

5. An Oklahoma Indian entrepreneur has enjoyed good sales from a car tag he designed that reads "RUA49R2" (Are you a Forty-Niner, too?).

are the old social love songs such as "Sweetheart Song" in this chapter. But the primary source of today's Forty-Nine repertoire lies in the contemporary generation of Native American traditionalist composers, many active in jazz and blues as well as at the powwow drum.

Not a newcomer to the Forty-Nine repertoire, the song "Ma ta Gi sso" has been around long enough to be remembered from the youthful days of some elders. The words "ma ta gi sso" do not simply mean "crazy"; Lenora Hart explains that the implication is that the girl in question has a bad reputation or is "loose" in morals. Some people think the song is somewhat naughty because of the title words, but Mary Armstrong has another opinion.

Mary believes that the point of the song is the defense of the girl by the singer. "Don't talk about her," he says, "because I'm going to marry her." In other words, the girl may have lived in a "crazy" or "loose" way at one time, but now she has changed, and the singer thinks enough of her to make her his wife. Mary's interpretation gives the song text a redemptive nature, reminiscent of an incident related by K. N. Llewellyn and E. Adamson Hoebel:

A loose woman among the Cheyennes was without social status . . . Calf Road, according to Black Wolf, was one such; a lost woman, but redeemed. She was a lass with more beauty than virtue. . . . When she disgraced herself, they cut her hair and turned her loose. She could get temporary liaisons with some men, but no presents were given for her in marriage. The salvation for such a girl was to throw herself on the mercy of an oldish, single man. If he cleansed her by giving a great religious ceremony before he married her, she became a respectable, if not wholly respected, matron. Calf Road got a [man] to pledge her a Sun Dance. Then she . . . renounced her past life before the tribe. Her champion danced for her in the ceremony. The priest of the Sun Dance prayed to Maiyun [Ma hi yo, God] to give her a new life. . . . After the Sun Dance for Calf Road was given about 1865, she lived faultlessly with her husband for many years. (210)

Mary's interpretation of "Ma ta Gi sso" as a song of redemption contrasts with other interpretations by those who consider the song to be somewhat ribald.

The song is presented here in three versions. The first (no. 20) is sung by the group of ladies present at Mary's house in Geary in September 1990. The second (no. 21) is Mary singing the song alone, followed by a rendition by Mary's daughter Rena Rose Young Bear (no. 22). Because the group song more closely resembles Mary's version than Rena Rose's, it is clear that, in keeping with customary Cheyenne respect for elders, the other women deferred to Mary, who also started the song. The difference between the mother's and daughter's versions is most noticeable in the rhythm, although there are melodic differences as well.

The group's and Mary's versions move almost entirely in groups of three; measure 10 is the only measure with two beats. The opening interval in the group version is a descending minor third; the interval is repeated in measure three. The importance lent to the derision interval by its repetition in the opening of the song matches the taunting name-calling of the text.

The others versions contain opening intervals encompassing a whole step; all other aspects of the melody are similar. An appealing aspect of the rhythm is the reversal of the eighth-plus-quarter (short-long) pattern established in the first four measures. At measure 6 the pattern changes to quarter-plus-eighth (long-short). In combination, measures 5 form a syncopated pattern that increases the song's forward movement; the pattern recurs in measures 8 and 9. Combinations of long and short are varied throughout the song, creating an attractive rhythmic elusiveness.

In Rena Rose's performance all measures have three beats. Her version treats the text differently, starting the second text line (Szi vi do do khi mo vo) an eighth note earlier than in the other versions and thus shifting the accent of the words. A comparison is shown below (accented syllables underlined):

Numbers 20 and 21:   <u>Szi</u> vi <u>do</u> do khi <u>mo</u> vo
Number 22 (Rena Rose):   Szi <u>vi</u> do <u>do</u> khi <u>mo</u> vo

The three versions' rhythmic uniformity returns at measure 16 ("mo vo") after only a brief discrepancy.

Number 23
"Ma ha Gi sso" (Old Man), Variant
Mary Armstrong, 9/18/90

1. *As spoken*

Ma ha gi sso, ma ha gi sso,
Szi vi do do khi mo vo,
Na do ssi vi sstoo mo.

2. *As sung*

Ma ha gi sso, ma ha gi sso,
hi yi ya hi ya,
Szi vi do do **khi** mo **vo,**
hi ya hi yo,
Na do **ssi** vi ssto mo **vo**

hi ya ho
[*vi ya hi ya hi yoy.*]*

3. *Translation*

ma ha gi sso	—old man
szi vi	—don't
do do khi	—talk about
mo vǫ	—her (him)
na	—I
na do ssi	—I will
vi sstō͡o mǫ	—marry, to be with

4. *Free translation*

Old man, old man,
Don't talk about (him)
I am going to marry (him).

*The last line of the song (in brackets) was reconstructed; the singer and listeners broke into laughter before it was finished.

The final version of the melody (no. 23) changes the opening of the text from "ma ta gi sso" (crazy girl), to "ma ha gi sso" (old man). Mary Armstrong heard this version sung by a girl at a dance. She relates the incident:

> At a Forty-Nine one time before my husband and I got married . . . this young girl—like I said, this young generation can say words but they don't know what they're saying—she changed this name "Ma ta Gi sso" and she said "Ma ha Gi sso," meaning "old man." And she was saying "Old man, old man, I'm gonna marry him, don't talk about him."

Mary sang "Ma ha Gi sso," but broke into laughter at the last phrase (mm. 20–24, marked "laughs"). The song has been reconstructed along the lines of the other three songs.

"Ma ha Gi sso" illustrates how easily song meanings can change in the oral/aural tradition, in this case by means of one misplaced phoneme (the letter *h*). It also illustrates how speakers of imperfect Cheyenne can influence change in the song repertoire.

SUMMARY

The social songs presented in this chapter are highly contrasting in sound, text, and context. The condition of humanity's awed impotence in the face of death is profoundly expressed in "Giveaway Song." The humor and the mystery of the ways of lovers is illustrated by "Sweetheart Song." "Ma ta Gi sso" reveals an earthy aspect, but deeper exploration with the guidance of an elder reveals a theme of disgrace and redemption musically explored in a few carefully chosen words.

These performances display a skilled vocal style that is neither strained nor strident. A rhythmic pulse is present in the songs, but the pulse is not vocally overemphasized, nor does loud volume seem to be a part of the aesthetic. These vocal qualities are in marked contrast to the sound of Cheyenne men singing around the drum.

Chapter Six

Spiritual Songs

SONGS ABOUT JESUS

While trying to find out what kind of songs were sung by Cheyenne women outside of a private ceremonial setting, I asked questions such as, "What kind of songs do you like to sing around the house? Do you sing in the car, or while working? What kind of songs seem to be the everyday kind?" Several had the same shy answer: "I know some hymns, but I guess you don't want those."

Why did this response surprise me? The singers seemed to think that hymns and spiritual songs would not be of interest to me. Perhaps they thought that, since the songs had Christian texts and sometimes European-influenced melodies, I would not consider them to be traditional Cheyenne songs. Their assumption is really not so strange, because many educated Oklahomans are ignorant about American Indian modes of worship.[1]

But hymns and spiritual songs *are* traditional Cheyenne songs.

---

1. The non-Indian students in my Native American music classes at the University of Oklahoma are frequently surprised to learn of the substantial repertoire of Christian hymns among American Indian tribes, saying, "I never knew that Indians were Christian!" As I take my students to hymn sings and church services across Oklahoma, they quickly discover the strength and influence of Christian beliefs within the American Indian community.

Cheyennes have been "Christianized" for over a century; it is only natural that Cheyenne traditional musical repertoire would include hymns and spiritual songs reflecting Christian beliefs. I assured the women who sang the songs for this book that all of the songs that they considered "everyday songs" and "songs women sing" were valuable and interesting enough to put into a book and to preserve for future listeners.

The women were particularly kind in letting me record and transcribe these personal spiritual songs or "testimonies" (stories about Christian experiences). The songs are heartfelt and intriguing in their variety, and they demonstrate both the continuity of traditional musical and religious expression as well as the singers' own contemporary innovations.

Four kinds of songs are presented here in the following order:

1. Songs that have existed in Cheyenne traditional hymn repertoire for some time, with monophonic texture and Cheyenne language text

2. Traditional Cheyenne songs that have been modified by the addition of an instrument capable of producing harmony and rhythm

3. Newly composed songs with traditional-sounding melodies, chordal accompaniments, and texts in Cheyenne or a combination of Cheyenne and English

4. European-American-style Christian hymn melodies to which Cheyenne-language texts have been added and that feature idiosyncratic vocal styles.

Some of the songs have corresponding variants in the hymnal *Cheyenne Spiritual Songs,* edited by David Graber. The songs recorded for this chapter, however, were sung from memory;

none of the singers read notated music. All have learned their songs by listening and repeating what they hear.

Every singer appearing in this chapter subscribes to the Christian faith. Some of them also participate in traditional ceremonies such as the sun dance or go to Native American Church peyote meetings. The women live by various personal doctrines, and each demonstrates strong spiritual values and enjoys a comforting and inspiring personal spiritual life. Like many Cheyenne people, these women do not hesitate to share with others the truths they have learned from their spiritual experiences; this music provides one way of sharing.

Number 24
"Baptism Song"
Mary Armstrong, 9/18/90

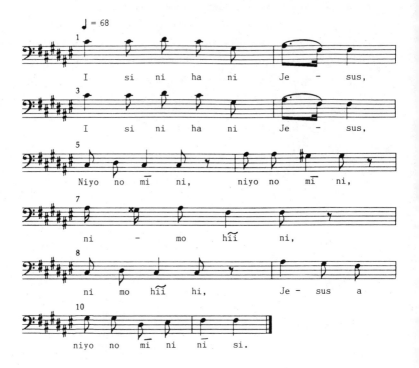

1. *As spoken*

I si̱ ni ha ni̱ Jesus,
i si̱ ni ha ni̱ Jesus,
ni yo no mī ni̱,
ni yo no mī ni̱,
ni mo hĩ ni̱,

ni mo hĩ nị,
Jesus, ni yo no mī nị ni nī sị.

2. *As Sung*

I *si* ni ha *ni* Jesus,
i *si* ni ha *ni* Jesus,
ni yo no mī *ni,*
ni yo no mī *ni,*
ni mo hĩ *ni,*
ni mo hĩ *ni,*
Jesus *a* ni yo no mi *ni* ni *si*.*

3. *Translation*

i sị	— our
ni ha nị	— friend
Jesus	
ni yo	— he
no mī nị	— calls us
ni	— you
mo hĩ nị	— come together
ni nī sị	— come (imperative); let's go

4. *Free translation*

Our friend Jesus,
our friend Jesus,
He calls us,
He calls us,
come together,
come together,
Jesus calls us. Let's go!

---

*"No mī *ni* nī *si*" is formed from the elision of two words: "no mī nị" (calls us) and "ni nī sị" (let's go).

This "Baptism Song," or "I si Ni ha ni Jesus" (Our friend Jesus), is a popular Christian song among Cheyenne people; it is also sung by members of other Oklahoma tribes. Mary Armstrong sang it during the September recording session in Geary at which her daughter Rena Rose Young Bear was present. Mary explained that the song had been sung originally by Rena Rose's great-grandfather Buffalo Meat when he was baptized. At his outdoor baptism, said Mary, Buffalo Meat received the song when he came up out of the water, and

> now everybody sings it—Choctaws, Cheyennes, Kiowas. He sang this "Invitation Song" and all his followers joined him and they were all baptized together. He was the chief around Kingfisher way back there when they were opening up the country. He became a chief—he had a band that lived way out, they call that little place Omega [pronounced O-mee'-ga]—no town anymore but there's people that lives around that area.

Mary's interpretation of the song is "He's calling us, He's our friend. Come on, let's gather." Frequently heard at revivals, it is probably one of the first hymns that Cheyenne children learn to sing.

The song also appears as hymn number 3 in *Cheyenne Spiritual Songs*. In a note on the song's background, Graber writes that the song was sung early in the 1900s by both Cheyennes and Arapahos.[2]

> This is one of the hymns that gave encouragement to young people far from home at the Carlisle Institute in Pennsylvania near the turn of the twentieth century. The variety of stories of the origin of this hymn attests to its popularity. Ova'hehe (Mrs. Bear Bow), one of the first Cheyenne Christians at Old Colony [south of present-day Weatherford, Oklahoma], is said to have been inspired to make this song by the ringing of the bells of the

---

2. Mary Armstrong provided Graber with the information on Buffalo Meat in *Cheyenne Spiritual Songs* (194).

Reformed Church near her home. Watan, an early Arapaho leader at Old Colony, sang an Arapaho song with the same melody, said to be the same hymn. Ho'evoo'otse (Buffalo Meat), an early Cheyenne Christian at Kingfisher, Oklahoma, is also said to have made this hymn as a "gathering song" for his people. It is believed to be the earliest Christian hymn in the Cheyenne oral tradition. (156)

Buffalo Meat was one of the leaders of the raid on Adobe Walls (see chapter 1), a battle resulting in his imprisonment in Florida. When he returned to Oklahoma, he became a farmer and a Christian, and the rest of his band followed his example. Graber notes that he was the first Cheyenne ordained as a Baptist preacher, and his descendants sponsor an annual social dance at Geary, Oklahoma.

Mary Armstrong's rendition of "I si Ni ha ni Jesus" differs slightly from the hymnal version, but the two melodies are easily recognizable as the same hymn. Mary's version contains a distinctive closing melodic motive missing from the hymnal version; the last five notes form a cadential formula sometimes found in European hymnody. The opening phrase resembles the first phrase of the gospel hymn "What a Friend We Have in Jesus." The song's format consists of three sets of paired phrases before the relatively longer last phrase.

Mary's rendition of the song reflects an old-fashioned gospel influence, with slides between the notes of its solemn phrases. The sound of nineteenth-century American Christian hymnody was incorporated into the Cheyenne music culture as early as the late 1800s, when missionaries held evangelistic "camp meetings" lasting a week or more. One of the best-attended was a Dutch Reformed church meeting held at Old Colony (south of present day Weatherford, Oklahoma), where this hymn is said to have originated (Graber, 156). This song is an example of traditional Cheyenne Christian music, with native text sung to an original Cheyenne melody influenced by missionary hymnody.

Number 25
"Ha hoo, Jesus"
Mary Lou Stone Road Prairie Chief and
grandson Jeremiah, 2/5/91

Number 25
"Ha hoo, Jesus,"
Mary Lou Stone Road Prairie Chief and
grandson Jeremiah, 2/5/91

1. *As spoken*

Ha hoo, Jesus,
Ni ya mi yo chi̱ mi no do̱,
Ni Ma hi yo ni vi do̱ və
Na vi shi̱ hi do da da no mo vī
Ha hoo, Jesus,
Nin shi va da mi̱ mi no ô̱.

2. *As sung*

Ha hoo, Jesus,
Ni ya mi yo **chi** mi no **do,** *hi yi,*
Ni Ma hi yo ni vi **do vi**
Na vi **shi** hi do da da no mo vī, hi yi,
Ha hoo, Jesus,
Nin shi va da **mi** mi no, *hi.*

3. *Translation*

ha hoo	— thank you
Jesus	— Jesus
ni	— you
ya mi yo chi̱ mi no do̱	— carry us
Ma hi yo	— God
ni vi do̱ və	— spiritual body; Holy Spirit

na	— I
vi shi̱ hi do da da no	— rejoicing
mo vī	— also
nin	— us
shi va da mi	— pity, mercy
nin shi va da mi̱ mi no ǫ̂	— have pity on us; have mercy on us

4. *Free translation*

Thank you, Jesus,
You carry us.
God's spirit makes us rejoice also.
Thank you Jesus,
Have mercy on us.

"Ha hoo, Jesus" (Thank You, Jesus) was sung by Mary Lou Stone Road Prairie Chief, who was joined by her four-year-old grandson Jeremiah. (His voice can be heard beginning at the segno marking). Jeremiah's nickname for this song is "The Mi mi' no Song," referring to the words in the last measure. Mary Lou teaches Jeremiah about Jesus as well as teaching him some Cheyenne language with this song.

A comparison of the first four measures with the final four reveals this song's return (ABA) form. Sixteenth-plus-dotted-eighth motives sprinkled throughout the song give a feeling of forward movement. The long interior phrase beginning at measure 6 contains six equal repetitions of B flat; the straight quality of the vocal style plus this repetition produce a tension that builds to a leap of a ninth to begin the third phrase (m. 11). The melody subsequently descends to a relatively restful B flat, and the repetition of "Ha hoo" signals the end of the hymn.

Mary Lou commented on the vocal style she used in this song and in other songs she sings. She referred to "a long time ago when they sang a real slow—what would you call it? A monotone? Where you sing it straight?" Her stretched, vibrato-free lines sound similar to the female vocal style in Eastern European laments.

"Ha hoo, Jesus" appears as hymn 109 in *Cheyenne Spiritual Songs* and is attributed to Frances Goose, the grandmother of Joan Swallow (see no. 1, "Grandmother's Lullaby," and no. 28, "Grandmother's Song and Story"). The first phrase in hymn 109 and the corresponding phrase in Mary Lou's version are quite similar; the interior phrases are different. The last phrase in both versions is a return of the first phrase; in hymn 109, however, the return is an octave lower.

A variant version of the hymn appears as hymn 131, also attributed to Frances Goose. The variant is much like Mary Lou's rendition and includes the repeated B flats of the interior phrase. Hymn 131, like hymn 109, ends with a repetition of the melody of the first phrase at the lower octave. All three versions of "Ha hoo, Jesus" begin and end on the same notes, with B flats and E flats throughout. This may be another example of pitch memory on the part of Cheyenne women singers, wherein the appropriate pitch level for a given melody is remembered specifically.

Number 26
"Heap of Birds' Song"
(Unaccompanied Version),
Imogene Jones, Mary Lou Stone Road Prairie
Chief, Joan Swallow, 2/5/91

Number 27
"Heap of Birds' Song"
(Accompanied Version),
Imogene Jones, Mary Lou Stone Road Prairie
Chief, Joan Swallow, 2/5/91

Numbers 26 and 27
"Heap of Birds' Song"
Imogene Jones, Mary Lou Stone Road Prairie
Chief, Joan Swallow, 2/5/91

1. *As spoken*

    Ni hoi̯ ni sshi va da mi̯ mi no̯,
    Ni hoi̯ ni sshi va da mi̯ mi no̯,
    Ni vi sshi̱ a mi o chi mi no,
    Nin sshi vī zz ta sto̱ zi̱,
    Na ho ha no ni
    Pī vi̱ sta no va̱,
    Nii ha Jesus,
    Nau gi vi ho ni̱
    O sshi va̱.

2. *As sung*

    Ni ho ni, sshi va da **mi** mi **no,** *hi,*
    Ni ho ni, sshi va da **mi** mi **no,** *hi,*
    Ni vi **sshi** a mi o chi mi no,
    Nin sshi vī zz ta **sto zi,**
    Na ho ha no ni
    Pīv sta no **va,** *hi,**
    Nii ha Jesus,
    Nau gi vi ho **ni**
    O sshi **va,** *hi.*

*The words "pī vi̱ sta no va̱" (good life) become "pīv sta no va" when sung.

3. *Translation*

ni hoi ni	— Father (God)
sshi va da mi mi no	— have mercy; pity us
ni	— you
ni vi sshi a mi o chi mi no	— You must carry us
nin sshi vi zz ta sto zi	— His love, compassion
na ho ha no ni	— we want
pī vi	— good
sta no va	— life
nii ha Jesus	— your son Jesus
nau gi	— we do
vi ho ni	— praise Him, name Him
o sshi va	— every day

4. *Free translation*

Have mercy on us, Father,
Have mercy on us, Father.
You must carry us in love and
compassion.
Your Son Jesus,
We praise Him every day.

"Heap of Birds' Song" (nos. 26, 27) is so labeled because two of the singers, Joan Swallow and Mary Lou Stone Road Prairie Chief, remembered that the song had been attributed to a member of the Heap of Birds family. Indeed, the song appears as hymn 120 in *Cheyenne Spiritual Songs,* having been contributed by Alfrich Heap of Birds: "Alfrich Heap of Birds, son of John Heap of Birds, learned many of the oral Cheyenne hymns passed down in his family. He arranged this beautiful melody, said to be from the Kiowa people, for his Cheyenne hymn" (Graber, 182). Mary Lou said that this song is heard at church services, revivals, and funerals.

The song appears here in two versions: unaccompanied and accompanied. The unaccompanied version has a freely expressed rhythm that is reminiscent of liturgical chant; the pulse is present, but not stressed, and the phrases swell and ebb in intensity. The song begins with a long phrase, which is repeated; the third phrase (mm. 11–14) has a lower tessitura, followed by accented slurred motives in a higher range. The words "Na ho ha no ni" (we want) are accented and even; another accent appears on the word "pīv" (good) of "pīv sta no va̱ hi" (a good life). The climax of the song occurs in phrase 6 (mm. 25–28) on the words "nii ha Jesus nau gi vi ho ṉi" (Jesus we praise you); the pitch level reached in the middle of this phrase is the highest note in the song. The denouement is short, descending downward, on the words "o sshi va̱ hi" (every day).

The dotted bar lines identify stresses within the phrases, with the first note after each bar line receiving stress relative to its surroundings. The song has no regular meter; the tempo is rubato. The range is broad, an octave plus a minor third.

The second version of "Heap of Birds' Song" (no. 27) is accompanied by Joan Swallow on the Omnichord. The Omnichord is an electronic instrument that resembles a chorded zither generally known by the brand name of Autoharp. In imitation of its acoustic counterpart's chord bars, the Omnichord has push-button chords; as opposed to the Autoharp, with its relatively limited chord index, the Omnichord has the capability of playing major, minor, dominant seventh, major seventh, minor seventh, augmented, and diminished chords on all twelve chromatic scale degrees.

The Omnichord was first marketed around 1980. The model used by Joan Swallow is an OM—84 Omnichord System Two. In producing chords on the OM—84, a player has several style options, including block chords, walking bass line, and "Sonic-Strings." The "SonicStrings" effect is activated by sliding fingers across the "strumplate," a touch-sensitive rectangle set flush with the top of the instrument; when played, the strumplate produces separated chord pitches in a variety of timbres.

Joan Swallow's choice of "SonicStrings" timbre has a celestalike quality. She uses a variety of strum patterns in each song she sings, including a thumb stroke glissando (i.e., arpeggio) and touching various points on the strumplate to produce individual tinklings.

The OM-84 has a variety of rhythmic capabilities. Like an electronic organ, preset rhythms have been factory-programmed into the instrument. These include two "rock" rhythm options, "disco," "latin" *(sic),* "country," "march," "tango," "blues," "swing," and "waltz." The tempo can be varied, and patterns can be coordinated with chords played on the push buttons. A block chord and a rhythm pattern can be played together. A walking bass (broken chord pattern with emphasis on the chord root) can also be produced. Because of the simplicity of experimenting with a number of options, the Omnichord is a useful instrument in schools and churches. The OM-84 can be played through an amplifier, and is powered by eight D-size batteries or a dedicated adapter (AC 124V to DC 12V).

Joan had particular reasons for learning to play the Omnichord. She and her husband are independent evangelists and pastors of a Full Gospel (Pentecostal) fellowship in Geary, Oklahoma. They sponsor a large revival each year around the

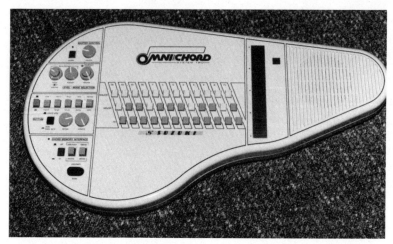

Figure 4. Model OM-84 Omnichord System Two (Suzuki Musical Instrument Manufacturing Company)—the type used by Joan Swallow. (Mary Jo Ruggles)

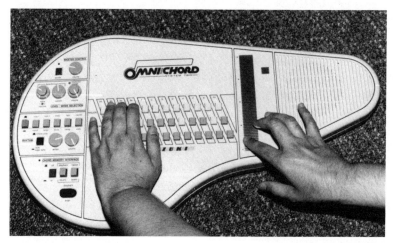

Figure 5. Omnichord with hands in playing position. (Mary Jo Ruggles)

time of the sun dance ceremony and also travel to British Columbia and other parts of Canada to evangelize. Joan is often
called upon to sing at church meetings, and she explained
why she bought the Omnichord for accompanying herself:

> Every time I get ready to go sing, if there's a guitar player he has
> to go "doing doing doing doing doing" trying to find me, or
> there'd be a piano, and nobody could play. [After buying the
> Omnichord] I locked myself in a room and I closed the door and
> I wouldn't let nobody listen to me. And I cried, and prayed and
> cried, and the Lord taught me.

Joan uses the Omnichord to accompany traditional Cheyenne
hymns and newly composed songs such as those later in this
chapter.

The accompaniment of "Heap of Birds' Song" effects a change
in the original song's rhythm, pitch, and phrasing. Whereas in the
unaccompanied version the phrases were free of strong metric
pulse, the accompanied version almost adopts the common-
time pattern programmed into the instrument. The song is not
completely in quadruple meter, however, notably at measures
11, 12, 15, 17, and 18. The chord Joan uses as a basis for beginning the song is B minor; there is a two-measure vamp from
the Omnichord before the voices enter.

Joan plays Omnichord using the "march" rhythm with snare
drum and cymbal timbres and a broken-chord pattern. Joan
also uses the "SonicStrings"; isolated chord tones are heard as
Joan touches or slides her fingers on the strumplate. The chord
changes to E minor at measure 10; other random chords are
heard (see "transition") before a return to B minor in measure
13. F-sharp major briefly appears in measure 14, then E minor
is heard from measure 16 until the end. After the singers finish,
the Omnichord goes on for about two beats.

In accompanying this song, Joan uses neighboring chord
buttons for sound variety rather than for their specific har-

monic functions, often touching various buttons surrounding the main chord. The buttons close to B minor are: E and F-sharp majors, minors, and dominant sevenths, and B major and dominant seventh. Joan keeps three fingers close to her chosen "home" key during an entire song.

These two performances contrast in an intriguing way, juxtaposing a traditional Cheyenne song with the same song accompanied by a twentieth-century Japanese-manufactured instrument with Western European harmonic and contemporary popular rhythmic capabilities. It is an interesting experiment in the combination of aesthetics; the Omnichord's regular rhythmic and tonal patterns form a difficult mold for adaptation of a song which, in its traditional state, has freer rhythms and a tonal system that is not consonant with Western European triads. This song demonstrates Joan's willingness to try musical experiments. Two of her original compositions follow.

Number 28
"Grandmother's Song and Story"
Joan Swallow, Imogene Jones, Mary Lou
Stone Road Prairie Chief, 2/5/91

Number 28
"Grandmother's Song and Story,"
Joan Swallow, Imogene Jones, Mary Lou
Stone Road Prairie Chief, 2/5/91

1. *As spoken*
_____

Ni ni i da mi no ni̱ i ha ni̱
Zi o vo vi no ni̱ Jesus
Zi kho do vi na do zi̱ ni so bi yo zhī ni̱
Ni ni i da mi no ni̱ i ha ni̱

2. *As Sung*
_____

Ni ni i da mi no **ni** i ha **ni** an,
Zi o vo vi no **ni** Jesus *a*,
Zi kho *i* do vī na do **zi** ni so bi yo i
zhīn,
Ni ni i da mi no **ni** i ha **ni** an.

3. *Translation*
_____

ni	— we/us
ni i da mi no ni̱	— depend on
i ha ni̱	— Father
zi o vo vi no	— giving first place
ni	— him (Jesus)
zi kho do vī na do zi̱	— testing times; difficult times
ni	— we/us
so bi yo zhi ni̱	— brings us through; pulls us through

4. *Free translation*

We are depending on You, Father,
We give Jesus first place,
He brings us through tests and
difficulties,
We are depending on You, Father.

The melodic basis for Joan Swallow's "Grandmother's Story and Song" (no. 28) can be found in *Cheyenne Spiritual Songs* as hymn 138. In the hymnal, the text is attributed to Belle Wilson Rouse (1903–71.) The melody is simply labeled "Cheyenne Melody"; Joan, however, states that the song was made by her grandmother, Frances Goose. Having learned the song when she was a child, she tells, in an accompanied interlude between repetitions of the song, about her grandmother as she translates the song:

> When I was a little girl, my grandmother used to fast and she used to pray, and the Lord would give her songs. So one day, she got me and she put me on her knee and said, "I'm gonna give you this song." And when I'm gone I want you to sing this song." And it means *Ni ni i da mi no ni*—"we're depending on you, Father in heaven." *Zi kho do vi na do zi*—"when you're going through hard testings and hard trials," *ni so bi yo zhi ni*— "I will bring you through." *Ni ni i da mi no ni*—"we're depending on you, Father above, to bring us through every trial and every testing that you go through in this walk of life that you take." *Ni ni i da mi no ni, Jesus*. "We're depending on you, Jesus."

While Joan speaks, Mary Lou Prairie Chief hums softly in the background with the Omnichord accompaniment.

The Omnichord is set on "march" and "auto bass synch" so that a "boom chuck" pattern is heard (see Omnichord pattern,

Figure 6, page 195).[3] The rhythm volume knob is turned all the way down so that the snare and cymbal effects that are associated with this pattern are not heard. Joan uses B-flat-minor, F-minor, and C-minor chord buttons and strums the Sonic-Strings. The tonic, B flat, is reinforced by the continuous use of the B-flat-minor chord; this causes no dissonant clashes since each chord tone is present in the song's tetratonic scale (A flat, B flat, D flat, E flat). Joan strokes the strumplate both with and against the beat of the music, sometimes upward, sometimes downward. As the pitches covered within the strums are unpredictable, in both frequency and duration, due to manual pressure variations and multidirectional stroking on the strumplate, this song has aleatoric qualities.

The song is transcribed with grace notes to reflect the stylistic swoops of the melody (measure 3, etc.). The vocal style is straight and strong, and the rhythm of the song is delivered solidly and without rubato.

3. On some other Omnichord rhythm settings, the bass "walks" on more chord tones than does this one; "march" walking bass is simply a repetition of alternating roots and fifths of the chord, followed by block chords on the offbeats, producing a "boom chuck" effect.

Number 29
"I Will Not Be Afraid"
Joan Swallow, 2/5/91

Verse 2

He - says   He will be - with me - -, He

says   He   will be - with me   -   - He goes before

me,   and is be - side me -   So I'm not afraid -.

Chorus 2

Ni -   a -   ma do va zi   - Ni - a

ma do va - zi   -   Ha hoo - Ma hi yo -

- Ni hi do   -   Ma hi yo o   -.

Verse 3

His - arms are un - derneath me — — His -

arms are un - derneath me — — His hand upholds

me — His love en - folds me — So - I'm not afraid

Chorus 3

— Ni — a — ma do va - zi -

Ni - a — ma do va - zi - —

Ha hoo — Ma hi yo — — ni hi do — Ma hi

yo   o   — .

Verse 4

His - word - will stand for - ev - er -   His -

word - will stand for - ev - er - - His

truth - it shall be my - shi-eld - and buc-kle -

So I'm not afraid.   Ni - a - ma do va - zi -

- - Ni - a - ma do va - zi - -

- Ha hoo - Ma hi yo - - Ni - do - Ma hi

yo   o   - .

Verse 5

He - will   give grace and glory —   He - will - give grace and glory   His cross be - fore me —   His ban - ner o'er me

Chorus 5

So - I'm not a - fraid -   Ni - a   ma do va - zi -   Ni - a   ma do va - zi -   Ha hoo - Ma hi yo - -   - Ni hi do -   Ma hi yo   o   o.

1. *As spoken*

Ni ya ma do va zi
Ha hoo Ma hi yo
Ni hi do

2. *As Sung*

Ni ya ma do **va zi**
Ni ya ma do **va zi**
Ha hoo Ma hi yo
Ni hi **do** Ma hi yo o

3. *Translation*

ni	— I/we
ya ma do va zi	— believe in; take refuge in
ha hoo	— thank you
Ma hi yo	— God
ni hi do	— we told him

4. *Free translation*

We believe and take refuge in you,
We believe and take refuge in you,
Thank you, God,
We told Him, our God.

"I Will Not Be Afraid" (no. 29) is one of Joan Swallow's first compositions, and she uses the Omnichord effectively in its performance. Joan describes her experience with composing the song:

I found [the words] in an old songbook, and I started crying when I read this book, this song, so I said, "Lord, give me the words in my language. I want a tune to this song—give me a tune, and give me the words in my language," and that was one of the first songs I got. And when He first gave me this tune and when He first gave me this song—I can't read music—I was in British Columbia, and I said to this lady, "I want you to listen to this," and I said, "I'm gonna sing this song, but it's a different tune, it's a Hebrew tune." And I said, "The Lord gave it to me, and He gave me the words in my language," I told her, and I started singing it, and she said, "It *is* Hebrew, it's a minor key," and . . . this one lady, she was a Jew, she said "Where did you learn the tune? Did you know that's a Hebrew tune?" And I said, "The Lord gave it to me."

In the songbook [these words] really caught my eye—in the songbook it said this song was widely sung during World War II in Communist China, and when I wrote it I started crying. . . . During the war people went through persecution—Christians went through persecution, and they had to give up their lives for the gospel, and here I complain [about things that are not important] and here these people said, "You either [reject] Christ or die," and [the Christians] were willing to give up their lives. It really touched my heart.

Joan adds an additional interpretation to the words "ni hi dǫ" (we told Him); she says it also implies facing God. This goes with the overall theme of the text: facing the future without fear through trust in God.

The recording includes Joan's adjustment of the Omnichord to her chosen tempo; the speed is increased from one quarter note = 95 to 106. Again using the "march" rhythm, Joan uses B-flat minor as her primary chord, with other chord colors mixed in for brief periods of a beat or two. When several individual chord buttons on the Omnichord are pushed quickly, the regular pulse is undisturbed, but the bass note and chord patterns change immediately; this results in unpredictable fluctuations of established harmonic patterns that cannot be transcribed.

No two verses or choruses are exactly the same; some are adjusted to accommodate the text. The form of each verse consists of two phrases that are generally identical in text and melody, followed by a rhyming couplet set to the melody of two shorter, similar phrases, ending with a short phrase in which the word "afraid" is present. All choruses have the same Cheyenne text and differ only in the lengths of some of the notes, particularly at the ends of phrases.

Figure 6. Omnichord pattern

Number 30
"Amazing Grace" (in Cheyenne,
Unaccompanied Version),
Imogene Jones, Mary Lou Stone Road Prairie
Chief, Joan Swallow, 2/5/91

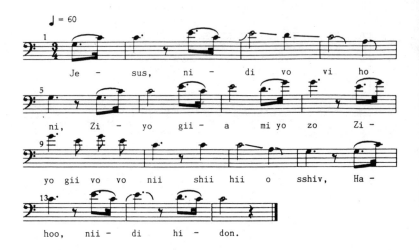

Number 31
"Amazing Grace" (in Cheyenne, Accompanied Version),
Imogene Jones, Mary Lou Stone Road Prairie
Chief, Joan Swallow, 2/5/91

Numbers 30 and 31
"Amazing Grace"
Imogene Jones, Mary Lou Stone Road Prairie
Chief, Joan Swallow, 2/5/91

1. *As spoken*

Jesus, ni dī vi vi ho ni̲,
Zi yo gii a mi yo zhi zi̲,
Zi yo gii vo vo nii shii hii zi̲
O sshi va̲,
Ha hoo, nii dī hi do ni̲.

2. *As sung*

Jesus, ni dī vo vi ho **ni,**
Zi yo gii a mi yo **zo**[*]
Zi yo gii vo vo nii shii hii
O sshiv,[†]
Ha hoo, nii dī hi don.[**]

3. *Translation*

Jesus	
ni	— we; us
vi ho ni̲	— praise Him
ni dī vi vi ho ni̲	— let us praise Him
zi yo gii	— because He
a mi yo zhi zi̲	— carrying (us)
vo vo nii shii hii zi	— takes care of (us)

[*]Spoken: "a mi yo zhi zi̲" (carrying us); sung: "a mi yo **zo.**"
[†]Spoken: "Vo vo nii shii hii zi̲ o sshi va̲" (takes care of us every day); sung "vo vo nii shii hii o sshiv."
[**]Spoken: "hi d o ni̲" (say to [Him]); sung: "hi don."

o sshi va	— every day
ha hoo	— thank you
nii dī	— let us
hi do ni	— say to (Him)

4. *Free translation*

Jesus,
Let us praise Him
Because He is carrying us,
Because He takes care of us every day.
Thank You, let us say to Him.

The first version of "Amazing Grace" (no. 30) is very much like the arrangement by Belle Wilson Rouse that appears in *Cheyenne Spiritual Songs* as hymn 24. The areas transcribed here with portamento marks between the pitches (mm. 3, 4, and 11) appear in the hymnal version with specific notes. The slides of the women's voices were less specific, appearing to reflect a country or gospel style. The song is sung in a very connected manner, with careful phrasing.

The second version (no. 31), accompanied by the Omnichord, displays two independent musical layers. The women begin the song, establishing a C tonal center and triple meter at a tempo of one quarter note = 56. The Omnichord enters in measure 2 at its own preset tempo, with the "march" rhythm pattern almost unrecognizable at a speed of forty-two quarter notes per minute. The chord used throughout is C minor; the pitch index of the vocal line, on the other hand, is a C pentatonic scale (C, D, E natural, G, A).

It is interesting to compare "Amazing Grace" with the accompanied version of "Heap of Birds' Song." These two songs have in common the juxtaposition of the traditional with the contemporary. What makes them different, however, is that whereas the accompanied rendition of "Heap of Birds' Song" displayed submission of its rhythmically free melody to an artificially produced duple meter pattern, "Amazing Grace" is able to remain aloof from the pressing demands of the Omnichord framework.

This can be seen by conducting a three-beat pattern along with the singers. The third beat is slightly stretched in every measure, pulling at times almost, but not quite, to four beats. In spite of the stretches, however, the triple meter perseveres. Careful checking with an electronic metronome revealed that, within measures 24–26, a compression of beats occurs caused by a slight increase in tempo (up to sixty-eight beats per minute at one point), but a barely discernable ritard in beat 3 of measure 26 stretches the melody back out. The original tempo (quarter note = 56) returns at measure 28.

The effect of the accompaniment added to "Amazing Grace" in Cheyenne is Ivesian; melody, and harmony, and rhythm operate in separate universes and yet are intimate. The performance is an example of true polymeter and polytonality, discovered in the unlikely environment of a Native American folk spiritual idiom.

Recording the songs in this book, the singers demonstrate remarkable memory and developed musical skills within the Cheyenne aesthetic. The women come from musical families, with grandmothers and mothers who taught them songs, sang behind the drum, or received songs as part of spiritual experiences. In "Amazing Grace," these women demonstrate an uncanny ability to conserve both pitch and meter; such abilities in children, to a much lesser extent, have been the subject of music education investigations on the topic of Piagetian principles (see Zimmerman). The capacity to function within this degree of musical abstraction might indicate that these singers have a sense of the way a given piece of music should sound so strong that no artificial device can improve or violate it.

Number 32
"I Have Decided to Follow Jesus"
June Warden Black, 2/7/91

Je - sus Ma hi - yo, ni dī vo vi hon I han Ma hi yo ni dī vo vi - hon, Ni di vo vi - yo Ma hi - yo - .

1. *As spoken*

I ha ni̱ Ma hi yo, ni dī vo vi ho ni̱,
I ha ni̱ Ma hi yo, ni dī vo vi ho ni̱,
I ha ni̱ Ma hi yo, ni dī vo vi ho ni̱,
Ni dī vo vi ho ni̱, Ma hi yo.

Jesus Ma hi yo, ni dī vo vi ho ni̱,
Jesus Ma hi yo, ni dī vo vi ho ni̱,
Jesus Ma hi yo, ni dī vo vi ho ni̱,
Ni dī vo vi ho ni̱, Ma hi yo.

2. *As sung*

I han Ma hi yo, ni dī vo vi hon,
I han Ma hi yo, ni dī vo vi hon,

I han Ma hi yo, ni dī vo vi hon,
Ni dī vo vi yo Ma hi yo.*

Jesus Ma hi yo, ni dī vo vi hon,
Jesus Ma hi yo, ni dī vo vi hon,
Jesus Ma hi yo, ni dī vo vi hon,
Ni dī vo vi yo Ma hi yo.

3. *Translation*

i ha nį	— Father
Ma hi yo	— God
ni dī vo vi ho nį	— let us name Him;
	praise Him
Jesus	

4. *Free Translation*

Let us praise the Father God,
Let us praise the Father God,
Let us praise the Father God,
Let us praise God.

Let us praise the Lord Jesus,
Let us praise the Lord Jesus,
Let us praise the Lord Jesus,
Let us praise God.

*In the last line of both verses, "vi yo" replaces "vi hon," perhaps owing to the downward slide of the melody.

"I Have Decided to Follow Jesus" (no. 32) was sung by June Warden Black at the El Reno Carnegie Library on February 7, 1991. June is Arapaho, but like many Cheyenne and Arapaho women, she has taken on the culture and beliefs of her "companion," the affectionate Cheyenne term for spouse. June learned Cheyenne from her husband's family while she was still a young bride, and now is active in singing behind the drum and at the sun dance. June and her husband taught Sunday school together, and she relates how the song came to be:

> The way I learned the song is that by singing all these church hymns, going to church, walking to church with all my little kids . . . and teaching Sunday school, God gave me that talent to put the words of this song together in the Cheyenne language. . . . I'll do the best that I can to sing the song.

The song is simple and direct in its message, and June's new composition became popular both with the Sunday school children and with other church members. June says that a lot of people sing the song now, and she is pleased to have contributed the words. The song both praises the Father God, I ha ni̱ Ma hi yo, and Jesus. The English words proclaim the intention to follow Christian teachings no matter what obstacles may arise:

> I have decided to follow Jesus,
> I have decided to follow Jesus,
> I have decided to follow Jesus,
> No turning back, no turning back.

June's interpretation of the full meaning of the song is, "Jesus, You teach me and lead me in the right direction, where I can follow. Don't forget about me, Jesus."

In the recorded performance, the pitch of the song does not settle in until the second verse. The song, which is thought by many to be an American folk hymn, is listed by Graber as

Assam, a folk melody from India.[4] Because the song was pre-composed, the transcription reflects the same key center in both transcribed verses, with idiomatic vocal techniques noted. June's vocal style is characterized by portamenti, and seems to have been influenced by country and western and gospel idioms.

During prayerful spiritual experiences, June receives original songs and prays for the same musical gift to be given to others. She perceives her musical talent, both for Christian church music and traditional Cheyenne and Arapaho music, as something not from herself, but from the spiritual realm. June has made other songs, but prefers not to record them.

SUMMARY

The contents of this chapter provide an overview of everyday Cheyenne spiritual music outside the realm of high ceremony. Unlike the context-specific songs of the sun dance or other traditional rites, these songs are appropriate for multiple uses: church services, funerals, revivals, children's Christian education, and individual quiet worship. Traditional songs passed from voice to voice take on new character as they pass through individual vocal mechanisms and are influenced by particular personal experiences.

These songs demonstrate various facets of a process described by David Graber in *Cheyenne Spiritual Songs:*

> When the good news of Jesus came to the Cheyenne people, many received it with open hearts. Those who introduced the "Jesus' way" also introduced their own melodies from their hymn-books. . . . Cheyenne adapted their voices to sing the new pitches

---

4. The same melody appears in *Cheyenne Spiritual Songs,* entitled "I am Following Jesus," with Cheyenne words by David Graber and Josephine Glenmore (Graber, 64).

and rhythms of these hymns. . . . A few people began orally arranging English hymn tunes using Cheyenne words. Naturally the pitches and rhythms of the English tunes were orally re-shaped into the Cheyenne way of singing. . . . Even after learn-ing English hymns . . . Cheyenne Christians continued exchang-ing melodies and songs with neighboring tribes as before, but now with words like "Jesus is really alive! Let's follow his way!" Sometimes the words of songs were translated by people bilin-gual in the native languages. Sometimes they were translated via English, or even sign language, but always via God's spirit. God has been speaking Cheyenne, not only in words but also in song and melody. (3–4)

Indigenous hymns and those with missionary roots continue to live side by side with contemporary expressions of Chris-tian belief.

Chapter Seven

Everyday Songs

CONTEMPORARY TRADITION

The singers in this book affirm Oklahoma Cheyenne women's musical heritage, but also make innovations as contemporary personal experiences come into play. These women enjoy American popular music as much as any other group of people who watch television, go to movies, or listen to the radio. But they also seek to preserve traditional songs as a part of their identity as Cheyennes.

The story songs, lullabies, and variants of the Forty-Nine song collected here illustrate variation, creation, and evolution. The Cheyenne music culture, like all music cultures, is continually changing. In Christian songs, for example, musical ideas have been incorporated from the Euro-American idiom, including functional harmony and major and minor tonalities. In addition, we see an electronic accompanying instrument imported from Japan. Among the singers, we see both those who keep the older songs alive as well as those who make new songs that are distinctively Cheyenne.

The singers in this book make their music among their own families, friends, and church groups. A decades-old record of a Cheyenne singing group featuring Bertha Little Coyote was produced to be sold to Indian listeners. Composer Joan Swallow has made no attempt so far to publish or commercially record her compositions. The singers found here are not concerned about public or commercial attention.

Whereas some American Indian tribes (particularly in the Northwest) evince a strong sense of exclusive song ownership, two incidents that occurred during the fieldwork for this book indicate that Cheyenne women do not share these feelings. In the case of "Heap of Birds' Song" (so titled in this book because the women who sang it referred to it by the name of its composer), the singers displayed no hesitation to sing the song, particularly since they knew it had already appeared in a hymnbook. During a visit with a group in which both Cheyenne and Arapaho women were present, I made a teasing remark when a Cheyenne woman sang an Arapaho lullaby, "Are you gonna let this lady sing an Arapaho song?" An Arapaho woman replied, "It belongs to the baby. It don't belong to no grown-ups, it belongs to the baby." Positive agreement from all the women present set me straight on this issue.

Songs whose texts or melodies were attributed to family members were freely sung for this book, sometimes with a verbal indication of "belongingness" that did not seem to restrict their use by others. Oklahoma Cheyenne women, seem to share a philosophy that everyday songs are, in general, free to be used by anyone, and whenever possible, the source of the song is to be identified out of respect for composers and their vision or musical idea.

The singers were very respectful of each other, gracious and complimentary of each others' musical abilities. When we would finish a recording session or interview, sometimes a singer would direct me to another woman, saying things like, "Go to see that woman. She really knows the songs." If someone discovered that another woman had sung a particular song for me, most of the time that singer refused to record the song again. Although I encouraged all the singers to sing whatever songs they knew that they would consider to be "everyday," there was very little overlap among the performances. Only the hand game song "Flying Around" and the Forty-Nine song "Ma ta Gi sso" were sung by more than one consultant, and both were done at my request and after some hesitation on the part of the singers.

I believe there are two reasons for hesitation or refusal to sing songs already sung by other women. Some indicated respect for the other singer's musicianship (even if she was not present) and modestly declined to duplicate the song. Others remarked how much better another person sang, thus indicating a concern that her performance might compare unfavorably. In spite of efforts to encourage duplicate recordings so that variants might be notated, most of the women politely refused to reperform songs sung by others.

All titles for the songs in this book were indicated either specifically by the singer or by implications from interviews. Labeling of songs (such as "Giveaway Song") or placing songs in chapters by type (war songs, etc.) was determined by singers' identifications of type and explanations of song texts and contexts. I had some preconceived notions about songs that might have existed at some time to accompany everyday work activities of the past (woodgathering, cooking, etc.) or of the present (farm work or other daily labor). Not one of the singers consulted knew that any such songs ever existed. One of the most elderly singers recalled chopping cotton as a child in the same fields as Negro workers. She said her family listened to the black work songs and enjoyed them, but she and her family worked silently.

While talking about some of the songs with different women, I noted some interesting responses. The words "hand game" or "hand game song" brought light to their eyes and lots of good memories of both recent and old-time events. Lullabies evoked tender memories of breast-feeding, rocking, and even diaperchanging. The words "Forty-Nine" or "Forty-Nine songs" brought a response that mixed pleasant nostalgia, eye-twinkling naughtiness, and sincere regret that the event has, in the opinion of most consultants, degenerated. Reminiscences of the romantic or playful times of young womanhood at Forty-Nine dances were often followed by rueful remarks on the present generation's activities at recent events; the general opinion among the singers was that Forty-Nine Dances unsanctioned by powwow committees or tribal police are not proper places for self-respecting women to be seen. These opinions, in turn, point out that the observations of all students of Cheyenne culture still hold true: Cheyenne women value chastity and respectable behavior.

Conversations with contemporary Cheyenne men indicate that they also continue to value the same virtues in women. Women are also valued as musical consultants by male singers. Several singers, male and female, remarked how men at the drum relied on the memories of the female backup singers and ask them how a particular song begins or what the words are. When they "help out at the drum," backup singers, or "chorus girls," also serve as a cohesive force in the performance of songs. When women make a surefooted vocal entrance during a song started by men, the sound of the drum takes on a special unified quality that inspires both dancers and singers. The high-pitched ululation ("lulu") of women in honor of the drum or a family member, or simply if musical excitement is high, adds an aesthetic lightning bolt to a performance; without women, there would be no "lulu."

The "lulu" is only one aspect of vocal performance that distinguishes male from female Cheyenne musicians. Whereas Cheyenne men often sing at high volume with highly stressed pulsations, the singers whose songs appear in this book most often sang with a less strident sound and with less volume. The rhythmic pulse of men's singing at the drum is stronger than that of women, although a clear sense of beat exists in every song in this book.

A remarkable aspect of Cheyenne singing (noted by Densmore in 1935) is a strong sense of pitch. Densmore found this demonstrated by Cheyenne singers who sang the same song with the same pitch index and tonal center day after day and in place after place. Current evidence for this phenomenon is shown in this book's versions of the hand game song "Flying Around" and "Sweetheart Song."

This pitch-centering principle is further illustrated by the singing of "Amazing Grace" with Omnichord accompaniment. There is also a sense of what might be called rhythmic centeredness. In song number 31, the triple meter of "Amazing Grace" remained essentially unchanged despite the accompanying instrument's electronically generated duple-meter pattern. Observations of pitch and rhythmic centeredness indicate that there are prescribed practices well known to singers of songs that, while leaving room for the personal imprint of an individual's musical interpretation, form the core of a particular song's identity.

In contemporary Oklahoma Cheyenne culture, women's involvement with music does not extend to the playing of the drum. Whether it be the powwow type, hand drum, or water drum, the instrument is the exclusive province of males. Nor is it customary for women to speak over the microphone at powwows or social dances, or to serve as masters of ceremonies at these events. Women do, however, advise emcees about the order of the songs and dances. They also have sole power to choose partners for the two-step couple dance, and men who would refuse to dance a "ladies' choice" must pay a cash penalty.

An area of music behavior in which women have been involved for some time is the making of songs. Cheyenne women composers were documented by Grinnell and Mooney a century ago. Some of the singers in this book also compose music and revise and create new song texts. One woman makes new songs, sings them into the air, and then prays that her songs will be "brought out" by men. (This singer, who prefers to remain unnamed, states that she has heard songs she has made come forth from singers around the drum who, she says, are unaware of their origin). From these contemporary examples we see that Cheyenne women are dynamically involved in the musical creation process, most often attributing their creative gifts to an ultimate spiritual source, called variously "Ma hi yo," "God," "Jesus," "the Holy Spirit," or "the Man Upstairs."

The principle of spiritual revelation as a source for song composition is a strong theme in Cheyenne women's music. The unnamed singer's gift of song, passed prayerfully to others through the spiritual realm, exemplifies both Cheyenne and Arapaho notions of music's origin. Mary Lou Blackbear's Arapaho spiritual song in Appendix A is further evidence of this belief. Joan Swallow's prayerful seeking of melodies for Cheyenne texts is connected to a tradition of musical expression resulting from spiritual visions. Her tearful beseeching of the Lord to teach her how to play the Omnichord is another example of the belief in revelation as the source of music and musical ability.

A theme flowing through my continuing friendship with and education by Cheyenne women has been the principle of "giving away." The significance of this Cheyenne tradition is reinforced by the length and profundity of Bertha Little Coyote's "Giveaway Song." In the acts of giving and receiving I engaged in while seeking advice from elders and consulting with singers, I found myself in the middle of a fascinating give-and-take. The meals, groceries, sewing items, cigarettes, and other gifts I presented I chose with care and with individual needs in mind. The amount of advice, knowledge, song recordings, text translations, and patient teaching I received was overwhelming and touching. I always receive, and continue to receive, more than I give. I was privileged to be taken as a sister by Diane Hawk, and I have found that honor both humbling and gratifying as I fulfill my duties as sister, in-law, "Auntie," and sometime grandmother at Hawk and Giglio family events and at the sun dance.

The prospects for continued study of Cheyenne music in Oklahoma are rich. The Cheyenne door of hospitality is open to those who respectfully inquire into the tribe's musical practices. Although ethnological and historical material is available in libraries, the value of firsthand information from tribe members cannot be underestimated as ethnomusicological and cultural preservation projects continue among the Cheyennes. Finally, the foremost goal of any non-Cheyenne student of Cheyenne music should be to give back to the people any knowledge acquired during a study. In that way, everyone can join the Cheyenne circle of generosity, a giveaway benefiting all participants.

Appendix A

Arapaho Songs

Mary Lou Birdshead Blackbear is an Arapaho married to a Cheyenne. The family lives in Geary, Oklahoma, and both she and her husband are active in the Cheyenne ceremonies, pow-wows, and social dances. Mary Lou, although raised Arapaho, has chosen to follow the Cheyenne way because of her commitment to her husband, James, who is a sun dance priest. Mary Lou is knowledgeable about both Cheyenne and Arapaho music, and loves to sing behind the drum. Her demonstrated vocal skill caused her to be one of the first women asked to be a consultant for this study, and she kindly consented. As well as backing up the singing of two other singers from Geary (Mary Armstrong and Rena Rose Young Bear), Mary Lou contributed two Arapaho songs during the recording session in September 1990.

Mary Lou was raised by her grandparents, who unfortunately were close to deafness when she lived with them. She could understand their requests, which were few because they were quiet people, but she never replied in Arapaho because, as she said, "they couldn't hear me anyway." She regrets not knowing the word-for-word translations of her songs, but she is able to provide interpretations and context information for both. The song texts have been transcribed using the orthography outlined in Salzmann's *Dictionary of Contemporary Arapaho Usage* as a guide.

The Arapaho alphabet consists of sixteen symbols, or letters. Of these, four represent vowels:

> *e* as in *nec* "water," for the most part approximating the English vowel of the word "n*e*ck"
> *i* as in *his* "liver," usually approximating the English vowel of the word "h*i*t"
> *o* as in *ho3* "arrow,'" approximating the English vowel of the word "b*ou*ght" but short
> *u* as in *núhu'* "this," for the most part approximating the English vowel of the word "h*oo*k" (Salzmann, 26).

An Arapaho consonant used in the two songs in this appendix that needs explanation is *c*, which sounds like the *ch* in "*ch*ur*ch*."

"Arapaho Pinching Song" (no. 33) is a game song much like the "Little Warty Lullaby" and "Tickling Song." Pinching hands are stacked up, with everyone breaking free at the end of the song to tickle and pinch each other "like bees," says Mary Lou.

"Come to the Father" (no. 34) was composed by Mary Lou's mother, May Whiteshirt James, who received the song during a spiritual experience when she was converted to Christianity. The interpretation of the song is: "All my people, come to where our Father is. I'm going there, I'm going to be with my Father. It's a good place, where He is." Mary Lou sings this song in memory of her mother, now deceased, and from it she receives comfort and renewed hope.

Number 33
"Arapaho Pinching Song,"
Mary Lou Birdshead Blackbear, 9/18/90

Ci ciu - bi - ya - te - ci ciu -
bi ya - te - ci ciu - bi - ya te -
ci ciu - bi ya - te -

Number 34
"Come to the Father,"
Mary Lou Birdshead Blackbear, 9/18/90

No he to he no hu, ci - wo te se - i,
No hu to te ku, no ho no we - ku - ho ne we - ko
te so no ni ni, no hu to te - ku
no ho ne we - ku - Hu ne he - to te se no - ne ni.

Appendix B

Cassette Tape Index

LULLABIES AND CHILDREN'S SONGS

1. "Grandmother's Lullaby" — Joan Swallow (A)
2. "Lullaby for Gray Eyes" — Wilma Blackowl Hamilton (B)
3. "Lullaby" — Imogene Jones (A)
4. "Lullaby for a Nursing Baby" — Bertha Little Coyote (C)
5. "Kitten Lullaby" — Mary Lou Stone Road Prairie Chief (A)
6. "Rabbit Song" — Rhoda Young Bird Braxton (D)
7. "Little Warty Lullaby" — Mary Armstong (E)
8. "Tickling Song" — Imogene Jones, Mary Lou Stone Road Prairie Chief, Joan Swallow (A)
9. "Mud Hen Song No. 1" — Joan Swallow (A)
10. "Mud Hen Song No. 2" — Imogene Jones and Joan Swallow (A)
11. "Mud Hen Song No. 3" — Imogene Jones (A)

HAND GAME SONGS

12. "Crows and Magpies" — Bertha Little Coyote (C)
13. "Crow" — Mary Armstrong (E)

14. "Flying Around"   Mary Armstrong, Rena
                                       Rose Young Bear, Mary
                                       Lou Birdshead
                                       Blackbear (E)
15. "Flying Around," Variant   Bertha Little Coyote (C)

WAR SONGS

16. "Soldier Song"   Imogene Mary Lou Stone
                                       Road Jones, Prairie
                                       Chief, Joan Swallow (A)
17. "War Song: God Is with Me"   Bertha Little Coyote (C)

SOCIAL SONGS

18. "Giveaway Song"   Bertha Little Coyote (C)
19. "Sweetheart Song"   Bertha Little Coyote (C)
20. Forty-Nine Song: Mary Armstrong, Rena
    "Ma ta Gi sso"   Rose Young Bear, Mary
                                       Lou Birdshead
                                       Backbear (E)
21. "Ma ta Gi sso," Variant   Mary Armstrong (E)
22. "Ma ta Gi sso," Variant   Rena Rose Young Bear (E)
23. "Ma ha Gi sso" ("Old Man"),   Mary Armstrong (E)
    Variant

SPIRITUAL SONGS

24. "Baptism Song"   Mary Armstrong (E)
25. "Ha hoo, Jesus"   Mary Lou Stone Road
                                       Prairie Chief and
                                       grandson Jeremiah (A)
26. "Heap of Birds'   Imogene, Jones Mary Lou
    Song,"Unaccompanied   Stone Road Prairie
    Version   Chief, Joan Swallow (A)

27. "Heap of Birds' Song," Accompanied Version — Imogene Jones, Mary Lou Stone Road, Prairie Chief, Joan Swallow (A)

28. "Grandmother's Song and Story" — Joan Swallow, Mary Lou Stone Road Prairie Chief, Imogene Jones, (A)

29. "I Will Not Be Afraid" — Joan Swallow and Mary Lou Stone Road Prairie Chief (A)

30. "Amazing Grace" in Cheyenne, Unaccompanied Version — Imogene Jones (Mary Lou Stone Road) Prairie Chief, Swallow (A)

31. "Amazing Grace" in Cheyenne, Accompanied Version — Imogene Jones, Mary Lou Stone Road Prairie Chief, Joan Swallow (A)

32. "I Have Decided to Follow Jesus" in Cheyenne — June Warden Black (F)

ARAPAHO SONGS

33. "Arapaho Pinching Song" — Mary Lou Birdshead Blackbear (E)

34. "Come to the Father" — Mary Lou Birdshead Blackbear (E)

RECORDING DATES AND LOCATIONS

A. Concho, Oklahoma, February 5, 1991
B. Calumet, Oklahoma, October 2, 1990
C. Seiling, Oklahoma, March 14, 1991
D. Kingfisher, Oklahoma, January 19, 1991
E. Geary, Oklahoma, September 18, 1990
F. El Reno, Oklahoma, February 7, 1991

Cheyenne Glossary

The following words are used in songs. An asterisk (*) indicates a word written in an orthography other than Lenora Hart's.

a mi yo zhi zi—carrying (us)
baby da hii sso—baby endearment; diminutive of baby
baby das—derived from *baby da so,* an endearing name for baby (as "Baby das *so* son *o ho,*" perhaps derived from "baby dass on," plural form of baby endearment)
da so—endearment
da va ni—are going
do do khi—talk about
do dōō—open
dô mi—are
do si—where
ga si—short
gi sso—diminutive; little
gii da i—endearing name for little boy
ha hoo—thank you
hi da niv—a man, mature
hi do ni—say to (Him)
hi hum mi—get married
hī ma zi—spouses; husbands
hi no vi dī no o—be brave; have courage
hi sso—diminutive
hii sso—little; diminutive (*vo go hii so*—little rabbit)
ho da o vi—kicked
ho do va ni ta ni—not difficult
ho hũ do—to wrap, as in a cradle

ho vi hi—nothing

hos ssta ha mi—threw me out

i ha ni—Father

i ho do—it is

i sī—it is

i si—our

ii via—flying, flying around

Jesus—same meaning and pronunciation as English "Jesus"

kī nii yo zi—tired

ma—when

Ma hi yo—God

ma ha gi sso—old man

ma i—red

ma i vi ho—red white man; German

ma mi das—added to *gii da i,* increases endearment sense of word; possibly refers to eye ("ma i khi") and big (prefix "ma"), therefore explaining singer's translation of "gii da ma mi das" as "little boy with big eyes"

ma ta—wild; crazy; loose

ma ta gi sso—wild girl; crazy girl

ma zi—turd

mi hi shi ī si—run for life, seek refuge

mi oz—smells

mo hū ni—come together

mo i hi—elk

mo i ha ni—magpies

Mo'ki*—composer of Ghost Dance songs interviewed by Mooney

mo ma o go in—condition of eye infection (*ma o*—red)

mo vī—also

mo vo—her

na—I/me/my

na—this, this thing, what (I'm hiding)

na do ssi—I will

na doo sū—I am going

na ho ha no ni—we want

Na ko vo sso—Bear Butte, the sacred mountain

na ni—our

nau gi—we do

ni—we/us; you
ni̱—him (Jesus)
ni dī—let us
ni di vi vi ho ni̱—let us praise Him
ni dī vo vi ho ni̱—let us name Him; praise Him
ni hi do̱—we told him
ni ho̱i̱ ni—Father (God)
ni i da mi no ni̱—depend on
ni vi sshi̱ a mi o chi mi no—You must carry us
ni vi do̱ vǝ—spiritual body; Holy Spirit
ni ha ni̱—friend
ni yo—he
nī o zi̱—sleep (command: "Go to sleep")
ni nī si̱—come (command: "Let's go")
nī mi o o̱—sweetheart; boy- or girlfriend
ni stoo—whistling, howling, blowing horn
ni vi—four
ni vi vo zi̱—modifies "hand game" to "hand-gaming"
nii dī—let us
nii ha Jesus—Your (God's) son Jesus
nii hii sto vǝ—death; dying
nin—us
nin shi va da mi̱ mi no ô—have pity on us; have mercy on us
nin sshi vī zz ta sto̱ zi̱—His love, compassion
no gi yo zi̱—alone; by yourself
no mī ni̱—calls us
no o si yo— handgame
no o si yo ni vi vo zi̱—hand-gaming
o va—except
o go gi̱—crows
o da khi ni̱—slit (eyes); Japanese
o va hi̱—all on earth, my fellow men
o sshi vǝ—every day
pī vi—good
shi sh gi ma—wart
shi va da mi̱—pity, mercy
sshi va da mi̱ mi no̱—have mercy; pity us
si sto vi—things

so bi yo zhi ni—brings us through; pulls us through
sta no va—life
szi vi—don't
va na do—difficult
vi ha no—flying around *(vi)* it *(ha no)*
vi ho i—white man
vi ho ni—praise Him, name Him
vi o zi—journey (such as to war)
vi shi hi do da da no—rejoicing
vi si vi vi—is there with
vi sstoō mo—marry, to be with
vo go—rabbit
vo vo ni o zi—surrender, give up
vo vo nii shii hii zi—takes care of (us)
voo zi vī—even though
ya ma do va zi—believe in; take refuge in
ya mi yo chi mi no do—carry us
yo zz zi—eyes
zi—they
zi do—this one (as opposed to *hi do*—this thing)
zi i vi—leave
zi kho do vī na do zi—testing times; difficult times
zi o vo vi no—giving first place
zi vi—don't
zi yo gii—because He
zo i ha o—they will fly

Bibliography

Albers, Patricia, and Bea Medicine. *The Hidden Half.* New York: University Press of America, 1983.

Baker, Theodore. *Über die Musik der Nordamerikanischen Wilden.* Leipzig: Breitkopf und Härtel, 1882. New edition, with translation by Ann Buckley. Amsterdam, The Netherlands: Frits Knuf, 1976.

Bass, Althea. *The Arapaho Way: A Memoir of an Indian Boyhood.* New York: Potter, 1966.

Bataille, Gretchen M., and Kathleen Mullen Sands. *American Indian Women: Telling Their Lives.* Lincoln: University of Nebraska Press, 1984.

Berthrong, Donald J. *The Cheyenne and Arapaho Ordeal.* Norman: University of Oklahoma Press, 1976.

———. *The Southern Cheyennes.* Norman: University of Oklahoma Press, 1963.

Brady, Erika, et al. *The Federal Wax Cylinder Project: A Guide to Field Cylinder Collections in Federal Agencies.* Volume 1, *Introduction and Inventory.* Washington, D.C.: Library of Congress, 1984.

Brown, J. Robert. "Plains Indian Women's Roles." *Whispering Wind* 23 (Spring 1990): 17–20.

Brown, William R. "The Art of Native American Music." In *Songs of Indian Territory,* edited by Willie Smyth. Oklahoma City: Center of the American Indian, 1989.

Burns, Robert I. "Roman Catholic Missions in the Northwest." In *Handbook of North American Indians,* vol. 4, edited by Wilcomb E. Washburn. Washington, D.C.: Smithsonian Institution, 1988.

Burton, Jan. "Norman Man Plans Tribal Ceremony for Warrior Son." *Norman* (Oklahoma) *Transcript,* 14 April 1991, p. 1.

Cavanaugh, Beverley Diamond. "Music and Gender in Sub-Arctic Algonkian Areas." In *Women in North American Music: Six Essays,* edited by Richard Keeling. Bloomington, Ind.: Society for Ethnomusicology, 1989.

Cheyenne-English Bilingual Institute. *I Speak Cheyenne, I Speak Arapaho.* Pamphlet. Concho, Okla.: Cheyenne-English Bilingual Institute, 1977.

————. *Ni zhi si ni ss zi.* Pamphlet. Concho, Okla.: Cheyenne-English Bilingual Institute, n.d.

Crow Dog, Mary, and Richard Erdoes. *Lakota Woman.* New York: Grove Weidenfeld, 1990.

Curtis, Edward S. "The Cheyenne." In *The North American Indian,* vol. 8. New York: Curtis, 1911. Reprint. New York: Johnson, 1970.

————. "The Southern Cheyenne." In *The North American Indian,* vol. 19. New York: Curtis, 1930. Reprint. New York: Johnson, 1970.

Curtis, Natalie. *The Indians' Book.* New York: Harper and Brothers, 1923. Reprint. New York: Dover, 1968.

Debo, Angie. *A History of the Indians of the United States.* Norman: University of Oklahoma Press, 1970.

Deloria, Vine, Jr. "From Wounded Knee to Wounded Knee." In *The World of the American Indian.* Washington, D.C.: National Geographic Society, 1989.

Densmore, Frances. *Cheyenne and Arapaho Music.* Los Angeles: Southwest Museum, 1936.

Dewitt, Donald J., ed. *American Indian Resource Materials in the Western History Collections, University of Oklahoma.* Norman: University of Oklahoma Press, 1990.

Dorsey, George A. *The Cheyenne.* 2 vols. Field Columbian Museum Anthropological Series, Vol. 9, nos. 1 and 2. Chicago: The Museum, 1905.

Dyal, Susan. *Preserving Traditional Arts: A Toolkit for Native American Communities.* Los Angeles: American Indian Studies Center, University of California, 1988.

Farrer, Claire R. "Singing for Life: The Mescalero Apache Girls' Puberty Ceremony." In *Southwestern Indian Ritual Drama,* edited by Charlotte J. Frisbie. Prospect Heights, Ill.: Waveland Press, 1989.

Forty-Nine. Audio cassette. Moore, Okla.: Indian Sounds, 1990.

Frisbie, Charlotte J. "Gender and Navajo Music: Unanswered Questions." In *Women in North American Music: Six Essays,* edited by Richard Keeling. Bloomington, Ind.: Society for Ethnomusicology, 1989.

———. *Kinaaldá: A Study of the Navajo Girl's Puberty Ceremony.* Middletown, Conn.: Wesleyan University Press, 1967.

———, ed. *Southwest Indian Ritual Drama.* Prospect Heights, Ill.: Waveland Press, 1989.

Gilbert, Henry F. "Note on the Indian Music." In *The North American Indian,* vol. 8. New York: Curtis, 1911. Reprint. New York: Johnson, 1970.

Graber, David, ed. *Tsese-Ma'heone-Nemeotòtse: Cheyenne Spiritual Songs.* Newton, Kans.: Faith and Life Press, 1982.

Grinnell, George Bird. *The Cheyenne Indians, Their History and Ways of Life.* 2 vols. New Haven, Conn.: Yale University Press, 1923. Reprint. Lincoln: University of Nebraska Press, 1972.

———. *The Fighting Cheyennes.* 1915. Reprint. Norman: University of Oklahoma Press, 1956.

———. "Notes on Some Cheyenne Songs." *American Anthropologist* 3 (1901): 312–322.

Hagan, William T. "United States Indian Policies, 1860–1900." In *Handbook of North American Indians,* vol. 4, edited by Wilcomb E. Washburn. Washington, D.C.: Smithsonian Institution Press, 1988.

Hart, Lenora. "Modern Southern Cheyenne." Department of Education, Southern Cheyenne and Arapaho Tribes, Corcho, Oklahoma. Photocopy.

Hatton, Orin T. "Gender and Musical Style in Gros Ventre War Expedition Songs." In *Women in North American Music: Six Essays,* edited by Richard Keeling. Bloomington, Ind.: Society for Ethnomusicology, 1989.

———. "Indians for Indians Hour Collection: 1943–1950." In *Songs of Indian Territory,* edited by Willie Smyth. Oklahoma City: Center of the American Indian, 1989.

Herndon, Marcia. *Native American Music.* Norwood, Pa.: Norwood Editions, 1980.

Herzog, George, "Special Song Types in North American Indian Music." *Zeitschrift für vergleichende Musickwissenschaft* (Berlin) 3 (1935): 9.

Heth, Charlotte. "Oklahoma's Indian Music: A Framework for Understanding." In *Songs of Indian Territory,* edited by Willie Smyth. Oklahoma City: Center of the American Indian, 1989.

———. "The Stomp Dance Music of the Oklahoma Cherokee: A Study of Contemporary Practice with Special Reference to the Illinois District Council." Ph. D. diss., University of California, Los Angeles, 1975.

Hodges, Daniel Houston. "Transcription and Analysis of Southern Cheyenne Songs". Ph. D. diss., University of Oklahoma, 1980.

Hoebel, E. Adamson. *The Cheyennes: Indians of the Great Plains.* New York: Holt, 1960.

Hoig, Stan. *Peace Chiefs of the Cheyennes.* Norman: University of Oklahoma Press, 1980.

Hyde, George E. *Life of George Bent: Written from His Letters.* Norman: University of Oklahoma Press, 1968.

Keeling, Richard, ed. *Women in North American Indian Music: Six Essays.* Bloomington, Ind.: Society for Ethnomusicology, 1989.

Laubin, Reginald, and Gladys Laubin. *Indian Dances of North America.* Norman: University of Oklahoma Press, 1977.

Leman, Wayne, ed. *Náévahóo'ohtséme/We Are Going Back Home: Cheyenne History and Stories Told by James Shoulderblade and Others.* Algonquian and Iroquoian Linguistics, Memoir 4. Busby, Mont.: Cheyenne Christian Education Project, 1987.

Lesser, Alexander. *The Pawnee Ghost Dance Hand Game.* Madison: University of Wisconsin Press, 1978.

Llewellyn, K. N., and Adamson Hoebel. *The Cheyenne Way: Conflict and Case Law in Primitive Jurisprudence.* Norman: University of Oklahoma Press, 1941.

Lowie, Robert H. *Indians of the Plains.* Lincoln: University of Nebraska Press, 1954.

McAllester, David P. *Peyote Music.* New York: Viking Fund, 1949. Reprint. New York: Johnson, 1971.

———. "The War God's Horse Song': An Exegesis in Native American Humanities." In *Selected Reports in Ethnomusicology,* vol. 3, no. 2, edited by Charlotte Heth. Berkeley and Los Angeles: University of California Press, 1980.

Marquis, Thomas B. *She Watched Custer's Last Battle: Her Story, Interpreted, in 1927.* Hardin, Mont.: Custer Battle Museum, 1933.

Marriott, Alice. "The Trade Guild of the Southern Cheyenne Women." *Bulletin of the Oklahoma Anthropological Society* 4 (April 1956): 19–27.

Medicine, Bea. "Warrior Women': Sex Role Alternatives for Plains Indian Women." In *The Hidden Half,* edited by Patricia Albers and Bea Medicine. New York: University Press of America, 1983.

Mooney, James. "The Cheyenne Indians." In *American Anthropological Association Memoirs,* vol. 1, *1905–07.* Washington, D.C.: American Anthropological Association, 1907.

———. "The Ghost Dance Religion and the Sioux Outbreak of 1890." In *Fourteenth Annual Report of the United States Bureau of American Ethnology,* vol. 2. Washington, D.C.: Bureau of American Ethnology, 1896.

Moore, John H. *The Cheyenne Nation: A Social and Demographic History.* Lincoln: University of Nebraska Press, 1987.

Nettl, Bruno. "American Indian Music North of Mexico: Its Styles and Areas." Ph.D. diss., Indiana University, 1953.

———. "Musical Culture of the Arapaho." Master's thesis, Indiana University, 1951.

Northern Cheyenne Language and Culture Center. *English-Cheyenne Student Dictionary.* Lame Deer, Mont.: Northern Cheyenne Title VII ESEA Bilingual Education Program, 1976.

Powell, Peter J. *The Cheyennes, Ma heo o's People: A Critical Bibliography.* Bloomington: Indiana University Press, 1980.

———. *Sweet Medicine.* 2 vols. Norman: University of Oklahoma Press, 1979.

Powers, Marla. *Oglala Women: Myth, Ritual, and Reality.* Chicago: University of Chicago Press, 1986.

Powers, William K. "Plains Indian Music and Dance." In *Anthropology on the Great Plains,* edited by W. Raymond Wood and Margot Liberty. Lincoln: University of Nebraska Press, 1980.

Remington, Frederic. *Artist Wanderings among the Cheyennes. Century Magazine,* August 1889. Reprint. Seattle: Shorey Book Store, 1970.

Rice, Darrell, ed. *Their Story: A Pioneer Days Album of the Blaine County Area.* Oklahoma City: Metro Press, 1977.

Risingsun, Ted, and Wayne Leman. *Let's Talk Cheyenne: An Audio Cassette Course.* Cassette album and booklet. Busby, Mont.: Cheyenne Christian Education Project, 1990.

Salzmann, Zdenek. *Dictionary of Contemporary Arapaho Usage.* Wind River Reservation, Wy., 1983.

Seger, John H. *Early Days among the Cheyenne and Arapaho Indians.* Norman: University of Oklahoma; 1924.

Service, Elman R. *Profiles in Ethnology.* New York: Harper and Row, 1978.

Smyth, Willie, ed. *Songs of Indian Territory.* Oklahoma City: Center of the American Indian, 1989.

Songs of Indian Territory. Videotape. Tulsa; Okla.: Full Circle Video, 1990.

The Southern Cheyenne. Pamphlet. " Anadarko, Okla.: U.S. Department of the Interior Indian Arts and Crafts Board, n.d. [after 1970.] Out of print.

Stands in Timber, John, and Margot Liberty. *Cheyenne Memories.* Lincon: University of Nebraska Press, 1972.

Strickland, Rennard. *The Indians in Oklahoma.* Norman: University of Oklahoma Press, 1980.

Titon, Jeff, ed. *Worlds of Music.* New York: Schirmer Books, 1988.

Trenholm, Virginia Cole. *The Arapahoes: Our People.* Norman: University of Oklahoma Press, 1970.

U.S. Congress. Joint Committee on the Conduct of the War. *Massacre of Cheyenne Indians* 38th Cong., 2d sess., S. Rept. 142, 1865.

Vander, Judith. "From the Musical Experience of Five Shoshone Women." In *Women in North American Music: Six Essays,* edited by Richard Keeling. Bloomington, Ind.: Society For Ethnomusicology, 1989.

———. *Ghost Dance Songs and Religion of a Wind River Shoshone Woman.* Berkeley and Los Angeles: University of California Press, 1986.

———. *Songprints: The Musical Experience of Five Shoshone Women.* Urbana: University of Illinois Press, 1988.

Vennum, Thomas. "The Changing Role of Women in Ojibway Music History." In *Women in North American Music: Six Essays,* edited by Richard Keeling. Bloomington, Ind.: Society for Ethnomusicology, 1989.

Washburn, Wilcomb E., ed. *Handbook of North American Indians.* Vol. 4. Washington, D.C.: Smithsonian Institution Press, 1988.

Wood, Raymond W., and Margot Liberty. *Anthropology on the Great Plains.* Lincoln: University of Nebraska Press, 1980.

Young, Gloria. "The Dream Dance and Ghost Dance in Oklahoma."
    In *Songs of Indian Territory,* edited by Willie Smyth. Oklahoma
    City: Center of the American Indian, 1989.
Zimmerman, Marilyn P. "State of the Art in Early Childhood Music
    and Research." In *The Young Child and Music: Contemporary
    Principles in Child Development and Music Education: Proceed-
    ings of the Music in Early Childhood Conference,* 65–78. Reston,
    Va. Music Educators National Conference, 1985.

Index